MW00467132

Books of related interest by Sam Hamill

Wen Fu: The Art of Writing (from the Chinese of Lu Chi)
Banished Immortal: Visions of Li T'ai-po
Facing the Snow: Visions of Tu Fu
A Dragon in the Clouds (poems and translations)
A Poet's Work: The Other Side of Poetry (essays)

BASHŌ'S GHOST

Bashō's Ghost

Sam Hamill

Broken Moon Press

The title essay originally appeared in *American Poetry Review.* All translations, unless otherwise attributed, are by Sam Hamill. Several of these poems and translations are from *A Dragon in the Clouds* (copyright 1989 by Sam Hamill, Broken Moon Press).

Printed in the United States of America.

ISBN 0-913089-07-9
Library of Congress Catalog Card Number: 89-61144

Cover print, *Way Nara,* by Kiyoshi Saito.
Used by permission of the artist, Fukushima Prefectural Museum of Art, and Carolyn Staley Fine Prints Gallery.

Broken Moon Press
Post Office Box 24585
Seattle, Washington 98124-0585 USA

to Keida Yusuke
to Kawamura Yoichi

and to Tree Swenson

with love and admiration

Contents

Preface

This is not a travel journal. While it is true there are records of several journeys within journeys incorporated into the "text," the text itself is the journey. Passionate engagement with the text includes a wanderer's knowledge of mountains and valleys, of the terrain of a subtext, in this case a subtext comprised primarily of great classics of Japanese poetry, the *Man'yoshu* and *Kokinshu*. As an aid to the uninitiated, I have compiled a bibliography of English-language texts which have, for various reasons, found their way into my personal library. It is not intended to be definitive, but provisional.

We begin with a visit to the great haiku master, Bashō, some three hundred years ago as he prepares to undertake a journey of his own. Along the way, we shall encounter Kakinomoto no Hitomaro, the great *Man'yoshu* poet a thousand years in the past; the Zen recluse Ryōkan, along routes he traveled nearly two hundred years ago; the great Modernist poet/sculptor Takamura Kotarō; and many others.

Because we are traveling in a foreign land, a country foreign even to modern Japan in many ways, we must learn a new vocabulary; but even in translation, it is a vocabulary which clarifies and enlarges our understanding and hence our journey. Searching for Bashō's ghost, we begin with Bashō; beginning with Bashō, we address his *forma mentis*, we learn what we can about his standards and ambitions, about his literary tradition, his imaginative ancestry. The first essay is a thicket of terminology and literary/historical data—necessary groundwork preparing us for a more relaxed journey later on, when we can look back over our shoulders at the beautiful, rich country we have crossed.

As we come into Bashō Country, we begin to see with fresh eyes that which was always there. "Knowing what precedes and what follows," Confucius says, "is nearly as good as having a head and feet."

Takamura Kotarō offers a poem of departure:

> No road leads the way.
> The road follows behind.
>
> O Nature,
> Father,
> magnificent father who made me stand,
> watch over me. Great protector,
> fill me with your spirit
>
> for this long journey,
> for this long journey.

Acknowledgments

The author wishes to express his profound gratitude to the Japan–U.S. Friendship Commission, the U.S. National Endowment for the Arts, and the Japanese Agency for Cultural Affairs (Bunka-chō), for a Japan–U.S. Fellowship in 1988. Special thanks are due to Shimamura Naoko at International House in Tokyo, to Aoki Shimpei and Marie Ohmura at Galerie Fine Arts in Tokyo, to the entire staff at the Nihon Gendai Shiika Bungaku Shiryokan (National Modern Poetry Museum) in Kitakami, to Christopher Yohmei Blasdel and Mika Kimula, and to our many friends along the road.

BASHŌ'S GHOST

Bashō's Ghost

> The moon and sun are travelers through eternity.
> Even the years wander on. Whether drifting
> through life on a boat or climbing toward old age
> leading a horse, each day is a journey, and the
> journey itself is home.
>   —Bashō (1644–1694), *Oku no hosomichi*

Bashō rose long before dawn, but even at such an early hour, he knew the day would grow rosy bright. It was spring, 1689. In Ueno and Yanaka, cherry trees were in full blossom, and hundreds of families would soon be strolling under their branches, lovers walking and speaking softly or not at all. But it wasn't cherry blossoms that occupied his mind. He had long dreamed of crossing the Shirakawa Barrier into the heart of northern Honshu, the country called Oku lying immediately to the north of the city of Sendai. He had patched his old cotton trousers and repaired his straw hat. He placed his old thatched-roof hut in another's care and moved several hundred feet down the road to the home of his disciple-patron, Mr. Sampu, making final preparations before embarkation.

On the morning of May 16, dawn rose through a shimmering mist, Fujiyama faintly visible on the horizon. It was the beginning of the Genroku period, a time of relative peace under the Tokugawa shogunate. But travel is always dangerous. A devotee as well as a traveling companion, Bashō's friend, Sora, would shave his head and don the robes of a Zen monk, a tactic which often proved helpful at well-guarded checkpoints. Bashō had done so himself on previous journeys. Because of poor health, Bashō carried extra nightwear in his pack along with his cotton robe, or *yukata,* a raincoat, calligraphy supplies, and of course *hanamuke,* departure gifts from well-wishers, gifts he found impossible to leave behind.

Bashō himself would leave behind a number of gifts upon his death some five years later, among them a journal composed after this journey, his health again in decline, a journal made up in part of fiction or fancy. But during the spring and summer of 1689, he walked and watched. And from early 1690 into 1694, Bashō wrote and revised his "travel diary," *Oku no hosomichi,* which is not a diary at all. *Oku* means "within" and "farthest" or "dead-end" place; *hosomichi* means "path" or "narrow road." The *no* indicates a possessive. *Oku no hosomichi:* the narrow road within; the narrow way through the interior. Bashō draws *Oku* from the place of that name located between Miyagino and Matsushima, but it is a name which inspires plurisignation.

This is not simply a travel journal. Its form, *haibun,* combines short prose passages with *haiku.* But the heart and soul of this little book, its *kokoro,* cannot be found simply by defining form. Bashō completely redefined haiku, he transformed haibun. But these accomplishments grew out of arduous studies in poetry, Buddhism, history, Taoism, Confucianism, Shintoism, and some very important Zen training.

Bashō was a student of Saigyō, a Buddhist monk/poet who lived five hundred years earlier (1118–1190); Saigyō is the most prominent poet of the imperial anthology *Shinkokinshu.* Like Saigyō before him, Bashō believed in codependent origination, a Buddhist idea holding that all things are fully interdependent, even at point of origin; that no thing is or can be completely self-originating. Bashō said of Saigyō, "He was obedient to and at one with nature and the four seasons." The *Samantabhadra-bodhisattva-sutra* says, "Of one thing it is said, 'This is good,' and of another it is said, 'This is bad,' but there is nothing inherent in either to make them 'good' or 'bad.' The 'self' is empty of independent existence."

Bashō, dreaming of the full moon as it rises over boats at Shiogama Beach, is not looking outside himself; rather he is seeking that which is most clearly meaningful within, and locating the "meaning" within the context of juxtaposed images, images which are interpenetrating and interdependent. The images arise naturally out of the *kokoro* or *shin*—the heart/soul/mind.

Two hundred years before Bashō, Komparu Zenchiku wrote, "The Wheel of Emptiness is the highest level of art of the Noh—the performance is *mushin.*" The art of artlessness, the act of composition achieved without "sensibility" or style—this directness of emotion expressed without ornament set the standards of the day.

At the time of the *Man'yoshu,* the first imperial anthology, compiled in the late eighth century, the Japanese critical vocabulary emphasized two aspects of the poem: *kokoro,* which included sincerity, conviction, or "heart"; and "craft" in a most particular way. The *Man'yoshu* poets were admired for their "masculinity," that is, for uncluttered, direct, and often severe expression of emotion. Their sincerity (*makoto*) was a quality to be revered. The poets of the *Man'yoshu* are the foundation upon which all Japanese poetry has been built.

Among the first *karon,* or literary criticism, in Japanese is that of Fujiwara Hamanari (733–799), author of *Kakyo-hyoshiki,* an essay listing seven "diseases of poetry," such as having the first and second lines end on the same syllable, or having the last syllable of the third and last lines differ. There were various dissertations on "poem-diseases," all largely modeled on the original Chinese of Shen Yo (441–513). The idea of studying craft in poetry must have caught on quickly because by 885 the first *uta-awase,* or poetry-writing contests, were being held.

At the time of the compilation of the *Man'yoshu,* very little poetry was being written in Chinese; Hitomaro and Yakamochi, the great eighth-century poets of the *Man'yoshu,* wrote without many allusions to Confucian and Buddhist classics, their poems drawing inspiration from the landscape and experience which is uniquely Japanese. Another court anthology contemporary with the *Man'yoshu,* the *Kaifuso,* represents the introduction of poetry written in Chinese, despite a few samples in the *Man'yoshu.* Through the influence of the monk Kukai, also called Kobo Daishi (774–835), the study of Chinese became the norm for what amounted to a Buddhist aristocracy. As founder of the Shingon, or "True Word," sect in Japan, Kukai followed a tradition of secret oral teachings passed on from Master to Disciple and had himself spent two years studying in China under Hui Kuo (764–805). The later influence of Sugawara no Michizane (845–903) established Chinese as the language of scholarly poets, so much so that upon his death, Michizane was enshrined as a god of literature and calligraphy. His followers found Japanese forms too restrictive for their multilayered poetry. Every good poet was a teacher of poetry in one way or another, many taking on disciples. Michizane's influence was profound. He advocated both rigorous scholarship and genuine sincerity in composition, his own verses substantially influenced by the T'ang poet Po Chu-i. The form was *shih,* lyric verse composed in five- or seven-character lines written in Chinese, but unlike the poems of most earlier Japanese poets, Michizane's poems were deceptively simple, and like the poetry of Po Chu-i, strengthened by a combination of poignancy and conviction. Poetry written in Chinese was called *kanshi,* and Michizane established it as a major force.

In his *kana* (phonetic alphabet) preface to the *Kokinshu* in the tenth century, Ki no Tsurayuki, author of the famous *Tosa Diary,* lists "six types" (*rikugi*) of poetry:

1. *soe-uta:* suggestive or indirect expression of feeling
2. *kazoe-uta:* clear, direct expression of feeling
3. *nazurae-uta:* parabolic expression
4. *tatoe-uta:* expression which conceals powerful emotion
5. *tadagoto-uta:* refinement of a traditional expression
6. *iwai-uta:* expression of congratulations or praise

Tsurayuki's list owes something to Lu Chi's "catalogue of genres" in his third-century Chinese *Art of Writing* (*Wen Fu*), which is itself indebted to various treatises on the classic Confucian poetry anthology, *Shih Ching,* or *Classic of Poetry.* Much of the penchant for cataloguing and classifying types of poetry is the result of the Confucian classic, *Ta Hsueh,* or *Great Learning,* in which Master Kung (Confucius) says "All wisdom is rooted in learning to call things by the right name," and that when "things are properly identified, they fall into natural categories, and understanding [and, consequently, *action*] becomes orderly." Lu Chi, the dedicated student of Confucius, reminds us that the art of letters has saved governments from certain ruin. He finds within the study of writing itself a way to set his own life in order. Studying Chinese, the Japanese literati picked up Lu Chi's habit of discussing poetry in terms of form and content. And from the fifth-century Chinese scholar, Liu Hsieh, drew the term *amari no kokoro,* a translation of Liu's original *yu wei,* or "after-taste." As a critical term, it would be used and reshaped, and used again, still a part of literary evaluation in the late twentieth century. Narihira says of a poem in the *Kokinshu, "Kokoro amarite—kotoba tarazu,"* or

"Plenty of heart; not enough words." Kuronushi says, *"Kokoro okashikute, sama iyashi,"* or "Interesting *kokoro,* but a rather common form." The poet strives for a quality called *amari no kokoro,* meaning that the heart/soul of the poem must reach far beyond the words themselves.

For Bashō, this most often meant a resonance found in nature. When he invokes the call of the little mountain bird, *kakkodori,* the name of the bird (a cuckoo) invokes its lonely cry. Things are as they are. Insight permits him to perceive a natural poignancy in the beauty of temporal things, a word identifying a bird-call—*mono no aware. Aware* originally meant simply emotion initiated by engagement of the senses. In its own way, this phrase is Japan's equivalent of William Carlos Williams's dictum, "No ideas but in things," equally misappropriated, misapplied, and misunderstood. In *The World of the Shining Prince,* Ivan Morris's study of *The Tale of Genji,* Morris says of *aware,* "In its widest sense it was an interjection or adjective referring to the emotional quality inherent in objects, people, nature, and art, and by extension it applied to a person's internal response to emotional aspects of the external world . . . in Murasaki's time [ca. 1000 A.D.] *aware* still retained its early catholic range, its most characteristic use in *The Tale of Genji* is to suggest the pathos inherent in the beauty of the outer world, a beauty inexorably fated to disappear together with the observer. Buddhist doctrines about the evanescence of all living things naturally influenced this particular content of the word, but the stress in *aware* was always on direct emotional experience rather than on religious understanding. *Aware* never entirely lost its simple interjectional sense of 'Ah!' "

As a more purely critical term in later centuries, *aware* identified a particular quality of elegant sadness, a poignant temporality—a quality found in abundance, for instance, in the novels of Kawabata Yasunari. In failing health, Bashō found plenty of resonance in temporal life.

Tsurayuki, whose own diary would provide a model for Bashō seven hundred years later, would ruminate on the art of letters during his sojourn through Tosa Province in the south of Shikoku Island in 936. In his preface to the *Kokinshu,* Tsurayuki lists several sources for inspiration in poetry, all melancholy in one way or another: "Looking at falling blossoms on a spring morning; sighing over snows and waves which reflect the passing years; remembering a fall from fortune into loneliness." Tsurayuki's proclivity for melancholy perhaps explains the general tone of the *Kokinshu*. This, too, is *mono no aware.*

At the time of the *Man'yoshu,* Zen was being brought to Japan via a steady stream of Japanese scholars returning from China. Along with Zen equations and conversations, they also brought with them Chinese poetics, which included a Confucian faith in the power of the right word rightly used. The attitude is paradoxical: the Zen poet believes the real poetry lies somewhere beyond the words themselves, but, like a good Confucian, believes simultaneously that only the perfect word perfectly placed has the power to reveal the "meaning" or experience of the poem.

Ki no Tsurayuki's co-compiler of the *Kokinshu,* Mibu no Tadamine (868–965), introduced another new term to the Japanese critical canon by praising a quality in certain poems, which he called *yugen,* a word borrowed from Chinese Buddhist writing and which was used to identify "depth of meaning," a character made by combining the character for "dim" or "dark" with the character identifying a deep, reddish-black color. But Tadamine used *yugen* to mean "aesthetic feeling *not explicitly expressed.*" He wanted to identify subtleties and implications by adopting the term. Over the course of the next hundred or so years, the term

would also be adopted by Zennists to define "ghostly qualities" as in ink paintings. But the term's origin lies within
seventh-century Chinese Buddhist literary terminology. As
an aesthetic concept it was to be esteemed throughout the
medieval period. An excellent study of Buddhism and literary arts in medieval Japan, William R. LaFleur's *The
Karma of Words*, devotes an entire chapter to *yugen*.

It was also the compilation of the *Kokinshu* which insti-
tutionalized the *makura-kotoba*, or "pillow word," in Japanese poetics. Although such devices appear in the
Man'yoshu, they appear with far less frequency, indicating
that they were not widely understood. But by the time of
the *Kokinshu*, most everyone was aware that "clouds and
rain" might mean sexual congress as well as weather patterns. The *makura-kotoba* often permitted a poet to speak in
double entendres or to disguise emotions; it was both "polite" and metaphoric. Along with the pillow word, the ap-
prentice poet also learned how to make use of the *kake-
kotoba*, or "pivot word," which would later become central
to the composition of haiku. It is a play on different mean-
ings of a word which links two phrases. It is virtually *never*
translatable. Consequently, when we read haiku in translation, it is usually severely "dumbed down," to borrow
Willis Hawley's phrase. The pivot word creates deliberate
ambiguity, often implying polysignation. The pillow word
and the pivot word would later become subjects to be reas-
sessed and discussed and re-examined time and again.

As this critical vocabulary developed, poets learned new
ways to discuss the *kajitsu*, or formal aspects of a poem. The
ka is the "beautiful surface of the poem," and the *jitsu* is the
"substantial core."

Studying the "beautiful surface" of the poem along with
its interior structure, Fujiwara no Kinto (966–1041) composed his *Nine Steps of Waka* in order to establish standards
based almost solely upon critical fashion. Certain rhymes

were taboo at a poem's closure. Certain vowel sounds should be repeated at particular intervals. Rather than a general and moral and emotional discourse such as Lu Chi's, or those of Tsurayuki and Tadamine, Kinto relies upon reasoned study of the architecture of the poem for his aesthetic. His critical vocabulary is that of the poem's structure. His anthology, *Shuishu,* has never enjoyed either the popularity or the controversy of the *Kokinshu* and *Shin-kokinshu.*

Zen demolishes much of this kind of literary criticism by pointing out that, seen from the core, the surface is very deep; inasmuch as cause leads to effect, effect in turn produces cause. A poem's "depth" cannot be created by packing the poem with allusions and implications—hermetics alone. Still, "surface" and "core" may be useful terms for establishing a necessary dialectic; they provide frames for reference.

As this critical vocabulary came into use, it was balanced by a vocabulary of the emotions. A contemporary of Saigyō, Fujiwara Sadaie, also called Teika (1162–1241), attacked structural criticism as hopelessly inadequate. "Every poem," he said, "must have *kokoro.* A poem without *kokoro* is not—cannot be—a true poem; it is only an intellectual exercise." Thus, by combining a vocabulary for the apparatus of poetry with a vocabulary for the emotional states of poetry, Teika believed, a poem could then be examined and judged. His insistence upon the true poem's *kokoro* returns the experience of the poem to human dimensions.

Another term in use at the time, *kokai,* expressed a feeling of regret after a poem, a consequence of the poet having failed to think sufficiently deeply prior to its composition. It was a criticism not often applied to Bashō, nor to other poets working in the Zen tradition. Bashō sought a natural spontaneity, a poetry which would indulge no regrets of any kind. Zen discipline is built in part around the idea of truth articulated in spontaneous response. A "correct" response to a Zen *koan,* for instance, need not be rational or logical. Bashō sought a poetry which was a natural outgrowth of being Bashō, of living in this world, of making the journey itself one's home. Two hundred years earlier, the Zen monk Ikkyū Sōjun wrote:

Ame furaba fure, kaze	If it rains, let it rain; if
fukaba fuke.	it blows, let it blow.

Bashō spent many years attempting to learn how to listen as things speak for themselves. No regrets. He refused to be anthropocentric. Seeing the beautiful islands off the coast of Matsushima, he wrote:

> *Matsushima ya*
> *ah Matsushima ya*
> *Matsushima ya*

It is the sort of poem which can be done once, and once only. But it is quintessentially Bashō, both playful and inspired, yet with a bit of *mono no aware,* a trace of the pathos of beautiful mortality. Simple as it is, the poem implies codependent origination, physical landscape, and a breathless—almost speechless—reverence.

Just as Bashō learned from Ikkyū, he learned from Ikkyū's friend, Rikyu, that each tea ceremony is the only tea ceremony. Therefore, each poem is the only poem. Each moment is the only moment in which one can be fully aware. Standing on the shore, he saw dozens of tiny islands carved by tides, wind-twisted pines rising at sharp angles. *Matsu* means "pine"; *shima* is "island." *Ya* indicates subject, but also works simultaneously as an exclamation. It functions as a *kireji,* or "cutting word." The township on the mainland is itself called Matsushima. Bashō entered Matsushima by boat in June 1689, so taken by its beauty that he declared it to have been made by Oyamazumi, god of the mountains.

Bashō walked and dreamed along the beach at Ojima beneath the moon of Matsushima. From his pack, he withdrew a poem written by a friend and former teacher, Sodo, an acknowledged haiku master. The poem describes Matsushima and is written in Chinese. And another, a poem in Japanese about Matsugaura-shima composed by an Edo doctor, Hara Anteki. The poems, Bashō says, are his companions during a sleepless night.

Two days later, he visited the elegant temple Zuiganji, founded thirty-two generations earlier by Makabe no Heishiro upon his return from a decade of studies in China. Bashō would wonder whether it might be the gates of "Buddha-land." But Bashō was no flowerchild wandering in Lotus Land. His journey is a pilgrimage; it is a journey into the interior of the self as much as a travelogue; it is a vision quest which concludes in *insight*. But there is no conclusion. The journey itself is home. The means is the end just as it is the beginning.

Bashō visited temples only in part because he was himself a Zennist. Temples often provided rooms for wayfarers, and the food, if simple, was good. The conversation was of a kind only the literate enjoy. Bashō, among the most literate of his time, seems to be everywhere in the presence of history. The *Oku no hosomichi* overflows with place-names, famous scenes, literary Chinese and Buddhist allusions, echoes called *honkadori,* borrowed or quoted lines, and paraphrases. But he didn't stay at temples during his famous journey; he rarely stayed at inns; he was generally and generously entertained by local *haikai* poets and put up by wealthy families. He enjoyed his celebrity and its benefits.

His literary and spiritual lineage included Kamo no Chomei (1154–1216), *Shin-kokinshu* poet, author of the *Mumyosho,* a kind of manual of writing, and of the *Hojoki,* an account of Chomei's years in a "ten-foot-square hut" following a series of calamities in Kyoto. Like Chomei, Bashō was deeply versed in Chinese and Japanese literature, philosophy, and history; and like Chomei, he enjoyed talking with working people everywhere.

After "abandoning the world," Chomei moved to the mountains on the outskirts of Kyoto. But his was not the life of the Zen ascetic. He made very regular trips to town if for no other reason than to listen to the people he met there. Reading the *Hojoki,* it is easy to forget that Chomei served as a kind of journalist, a deeply compassionate witness to the incredible suffering of people during his lifetime. Chomei's world was shaken to the core when winds spread a great fire through Kyoto, leveling a third of the capital city in 1177. In 1181, a famine began which lasted two years. Those and other calamities informed Chomei's deep sense of compassion. Just as a disciple of Sakyamuni, Vimalakirti, served as a model for Chomei's retreat, Bashō found in Chomei a model for compassionate engagement with others. Chomei had written, "Trivial things spoken along the way enliven the faith of my awakened heart."

Chomei's interest in people in general was a trait Bashō shared. And unlike Saigyō, Kamo no Chomei could not separate his life from his art. Bashō enjoyed the possibility of making a living from the writing of haiku, and therefore his art and life were indeed one. He also felt a deep connection to history. He speaks as though all eternity were only yesterday, each memory vivid, the historical figures themselves almost contemporary; he speaks confidentially, expecting his reader to be versed in details so that his own brief journal may serve to call up enormous resonances, ghosts at every turn. But Bashō doesn't "pack" his lines with references. His subjects and his knowledge flow freely, almost casually, through his writing.

Chomei bears witness to countless thousands of deaths after the great fire swept Kyoto, and says, "They die in the morning and are born in the evening like bubbles

on water." Bashō walks across the plain where a great battle once raged. Only empty fields remain. The landscape
reminds him of a poem by Tu Fu (712–770) in which the
T'ang poet surveyed a similar scene and wrote,

> The whole country devastated,
> only mountains and rivers remain.
> In springtime, at the ruined castle,
> the grass is always green.

For Bashō, the grass blowing in the breeze seems especially poignant, so much so that his eyes well into tears. If
Tu Fu, both as a poet and as a man, is a fit model—to be em-
ulated rather than copied—Bashō is reminded of how little
we have learned from all our interminable warfare and
bloodshed. The wind blows. The grasses bend. Bashō
moistens his brush months later and writes, remembering,

Natsugusa ya	Summer grasses—
tsuwamono domo ga	after great soldiers'
yume no ato	imperial dreams.

His echo of Tu Fu underscores the profound irony. For
Bashō, the journey into the interior of the way of poetry
had been long and arduous. His simple "summer grasses"
haiku carried within it the sort of resonance he sought. The
grasses with their plethora of associations, the ghosts of Hi-
dehira, Yoritomo, and Yoshitsune, an allusion drawn from
a famous Noh drama—Bashō framed his verse with rich
and complex historical, literary, and philosophical associations. The poem implies that the grasses are the only consequence of the warriors' dreams, that the grasses are all that
remains, a Buddhist parallel to the Bible's "dust into dust,"
the accompanying prose drawing the reader into a vast net-
work of allusion.

The haiku itself is spare, clean, swift as a boning knife.
The melopoeia combines *a, o,* and *u* sounds: *tsu, gu* in line
1; *tsu* and *yu* in lines 2 and 3; the *tsu* sound is very quick,

almost to the point of silence. The *a* sound punctuates the whole poem: *na, sa, ya* among the five syllables of line 1; *wa* and *ga* among the seven syllables of line 2, the four remaining being *mono* and *domo;* and a semiconcluding *a* before *to.* Among the seventeen syllables are six *a* syllables, six *o* syllables, and four *u* syllables.

The Western reader, accustomed to being conscious of reading translation and having fallen into the slothful and unrewarding habit of reading poetry silently, often misses Bashō's ear by neglecting the *Romaji,* or "Romanized" Japanese, so frequently printed with the poems. Onomatopoeia, rhyme, and slant rhyme are Bashō's favorite tools, and he uses them like no one else in Japanese literature. He wrote from within the body; his poems are full of breath and sound as well as images and allusions.

What Bashō read, he read deeply and attentively. As a poet, he had blossomed slowly, ever-changing, constantly learning. The poetry of his twenties and thirties is competent and generally undistinguished. It is the learned poetry of received ideas composed by a good mind. It lacks breadth and depth of vision. But his interest in Chinese poetry continued to grow. He studied Tu Fu (Toho in Japanese) assiduously during his twenties and thirties, and he read Li T'ai-po (Rihaku in Japanese). Along with the Chinese poets, he traveled with a copy of *Chuang Tzu.* He seems to have struggled with Zen discipline and Chinese poetry and philosophy all during his thirties, and the result was a poetry at first clearly derivative, but later becoming more his own as he grew into his studies. Upon entering his forties, Bashō's verse changed. He learned to be comfortable with his teachers and with his own scholarship. His Zen practice had steadied his vision. Fewer aspirations stood in his way.

Born in 1644 in Ueno, Iga Province, approximately thirty miles southeast from Kyoto, the son of Matsuo Yozaemon, a low-ranking samurai, Bashō had at least one elder brother and four sisters. As a young man, he served in the household of a higher-ranking local samurai, Todo Shinshichiro, becoming a companion to his son, Yoshitada, whose "haiku name" was Sengin. Bashō often joined his master in composing the linked verses called *haikai,* but was still known by his samurai name, Matsuo Munefusa, despite having taken his first haiku name, Sobo. Bashō also had a common-law wife at this time, Jutei, who later became a nun. And although there is little verifiable information on these years, Bashō seems to have experimented a good deal. He would later say upon reflection, "I at one time coveted an official post," and "There was a time when I became fascinated with the ways of homosexual love."

Whether because of a complicated love-life or as a result of the death of his friend and master, Sengin, Bashō apparently simply wandered off sometime around 1667, leaving behind his samurai name and position. It was not unique for a man like Bashō to leave samurai society. Many who did so became monks. Some early biographies claim he went to Kyoto to study philosophy, poetry, and calligraphy. He re-emerged in 1672 as editor and commentator on a volume of haikai, *The Seashell Game* (*Kai Oi*). With contributions from about thirty poets, *The Seashell Game* shows Bashō to be witty, deeply knowledgeable, and rather light-hearted. It was well-enough received to encourage him to move to Edo (present-day Tokyo).

While it is not clear whether he made his living in Edo working as a haiku poet and teacher, Bashō does tell us that those first years in the growing city were not easy ones. He would later recall that he was torn between the desire to become a great poet and the desire to simply give up verse altogether. But his verse was, in many ways, his life. He continued to study and to write. And he continued to attract students, a number of whom were, like himself, drop-outs from samurai or *bushido* society who also rejected the vulgar

values of the class below the samurai, the *chonin,* or urban
merchant class. Bashō believed literature provided an alter-
native set of values which he called *fuga no michi,* "the way
of elegance." He claimed that his life was stitched together
by "the single thread of art," which permitted him to follow
"no religious law" and no popular customs.

Robert Aitken's study of Bashō, *A Zen Wave,* draws
many parallels between Bashō's attitude and Zen poetics.
But it is mistaken to think Bashō retreated into Buddhism.
He admired the Zen mind; the "Buddhism" attached to Zen
was, to him, almost superfluous. And he did, during his
years in Edo, study Zen under the priest Butchō (1642–
1715), apparently even to the point of considering the mo-
nastic life, but whether to escape from decadent culture or
as a philosophical passion remains unclear. Despite his abil-
ity to attract students, he seems to have spent much of the
time in a state of perpetual despondency, loneliness everywhere crowding in on him. No doubt this state of mind was
compounded as a result of chronically poor health, but
Bashō was also engaging true *sabishi,* a spiritual "loneliness" which served haikai culture in much the same way *mu,*
or "nothingness," served Zen. Achieving true spiritual
poverty, true inner emptiness, everything becomes our
own. This is a path leading directly toward selflessness, toward *kensho,* or "enlightenment."

In the winter of 1680, his students built him a small hut
where he could establish a permanent home. In the spring,
someone planted a banana (or *bashō*) tree in the yard, giving
the hut, "Bashō-an," its name, and the poet a new *nom de
plume.* Bashō-an burned to the ground when a fire swept
through the neighborhood in the winter of 1682. Friends
and disciples built a new Bashō-an during the winter of
1683. His disciples were also beginning to earn names of
their own. Bashō wrote of one, Kikaku, that his poems con-
tained the "spiritual broth" of Tu Fu. But his followers

were also time-consuming. And there were suddenly disciples *of* his disciples, literally hundreds of "Bashō group" poets springing up. More and more projects were offered for his possible participation. He longed for quietude.

During 1684 and early 1685, the poet traveled to Kyoto, Nara, and his old home in Ueno, and composed *Journey of a Weather-beaten Skeleton,* the first of his travel journals and one notable for its constant pathos. His mother had died in Ueno. The trip was a long eight months, arduous and extremely dangerous. The forty-year-old poet had spent thirty years in Iga and a decade in Edo before beginning the wanderer's life for which he became so famous. Donald Keene has said this first travel journal reads as though it were translated from Chinese, allusions and parallels drawn from Ch'an (Zen) literature in nearly every line. Bashō was struggling to achieve a resonance between the fleeting moment and the eternal, between the instant of awareness and the vast endless Void of Zen.

In 1687, he traveled with his friend, Sora, and a Zen monk to Kashima Shrine, fifty miles east of Edo, where, among other things, Bashō visited his Zen master, Butchō, who had retired there. His record of this trip, *A Visit to Kashima Shrine,* is very brief, as is his *Visit to Sarashina Village,* each the result of a short "moon-viewing" journey to a rustic setting. At Kashima, they were greeted by a rainstorm, but at Sarashina, Bashō watched the moon rise through the trees, offered a toast with his companions, and was given a cup by the innkeeper, a cup which caught his attention: "The innkeeper brought us cups that were larger than usual, with crude lacquer designs. . . . I was fascinated with those cups . . . and it was because of the locale."

Bashō, after flirting with dense Chinese diction, was turning toward *sabi,* an elegant simplicity tinged with the flavor of loneliness. *Sabi* comes from the more pure "loneliness" of *sabishi.* It was an idea which fit perfectly with his

notion of *fuga no michi,* "the way of elegance," together
with his rejection of bourgeois society. Elegant simplicity.
Visiting the rustic village of Sarashina to view the moon,
the poet is given a cup by an innkeeper, and he examines it
closely by moonlight and lamplight, his imagination held
captive by the working hands of some villager. His idea of
sabi has about it elements of *yugen, mono no aware,* and
plenty of *kokoro.* His poetry, so indebted to Japanese and
Chinese classics, could be simplified, he could find a poetry
which would leave the reader with a sense of *sabi.* Perhaps
he had followed classical Chinese rhetorical conventions a
bit too closely. He wanted to make images which positively
radiated with reality. He turned the sake cup in his hand, and
as he did so, his mind turned.

During his years of Zen training, he had spoken of striv-
ing to achieve the "religious flavor" of the poetry of Han
Shan (Kanzan in Japanese, Cold Mountain in English); he
had wanted to "clothe in Japanese language" the poetry of
Po Chu-i. But in *A Visit to Kashima Shrine,* he chose a far
simpler syntax, writing almost exclusively in *kana,* the Japanese phonetic alphabet, rather than in *kanji,* or Chinese
written characters.

In late 1687, Bashō had made another journey, visiting
Ise, Nagoya, Iga, Yoshino, and Nara, traveling with a disciple who had been exiled. The writing from this journey
would not be published until 1709, more than ten years after
the poet's death. Scholars date completion of the *Manuscript
in My Knapsack (Oi no kobumi)* at about 1691, the same time
the poet was writing *Oku no hosomichi.* He says in the *Knapsack* manuscript that "Nobody has succeeded in making any
improvement in travel diaries since Ki no Tsurayuki,
Chomei, and the nun Abutsu ... the rest have merely imi-
tated." Clearly, he was searching for a style which could
reinvigorate an ancient form. He must have felt that he had
gained a powerful knowledge which only a simple style

could accommodate. He also said in the *Knapsack* manuscript, "Saigyō's waka, Sogi's renga,/ Sesshu's sumi, Rikyu's tea,— / the spirit which moves them is one spirit."

Whether he had arrived at his mature style by that early morning in late March 1689, he was eager to begin his journey north to Sendai and on to Hiraizumi, where the Fujiwara clan had flourished and perished. He would then push west, cross the mountains, turn south down the west coast of Honshu, then turn east again toward Ise, the vast majority of the trip made on foot. He left behind the idiosyncrasies and frivolities of the Teitoku and Danrin schools of haikai. He left perhaps as many as sixty students of the Bashō School who, in turn, were acquiring students of their own.

When his disciple, Kikaku, overpraised a Bashō image of a cold fish on a fishmonger's shelf, saying he had attained "mystery and depth," Bashō replied that what he most valued was the poem's "ordinariness." He had come almost full circle from the densely allusive Chinese style into a truly elegant simplicity which was in no way frivolous. He had elevated the haikai from word-play into lyric poetry, from a game played by poetasters into a spiritual dimension. "Abide by rules," Bashō said, "then throw them out!— only *then* may you achieve true freedom." Bashō's freedom expressed itself by redefining haiku as a complete thing, a full lyric form capable of handling complex data and emotional depth and spiritual seriousness while still retaining some element of playfulness.

Confucius says, "Only the one who attains perfect sincerity under Heaven may discover one's 'true nature.' One who accomplishes this participates fully in the transformation of Heaven and Earth, and being fully human, becomes with them a third thing." Knowing this, Bashō tells his students, "Do not simply follow the footsteps of the Ancients; seek what they sought." In order to avoid simply

filling the ancient footsteps of his predecessors, Bashō studies them assiduously, attentively. And when he has had his
fill of ancient poets and students and the infinite dialectic
that is literature and art, when his heart is filled with wan-
derlust, he chooses a traveling companion, fills a small pack
with essentials—and, of course, a few *hanamuke*—and
walks off into the dawn, into history, into the geography of
the soul which makes the journey home.

In Ryōkan Country

It is the first week of May—"Golden Week"—and most of Japan is on vacation. The *sakura zensen,* or "cherry blossom line," has been moving steadily north and is just arriving in Niigata Prefecture on the northwestern side of Honshu. People from towns and villages of the Japan Alps celebrate cherry blossom time with great enthusiasm, as has all of Japan for more than a thousand years, finding in the brief lifespan of pale pink and white blossoms a touching symbol for our own precarious and temporal lives. This has been so since before the time of the *Man'yoshu.*

Three hundred years ago, Bashō wrote:

Ki no moto ni	From all these trees—
shiru mo namasu mo	in salads, soups,
sakura kana	everywhere—
	cherry blossoms fall.

It is all too easy to understand such a poem at only its most trivial level. Bashō provides no literary comparison in his poem; rather, he engages the reader with the blossoms themselves, with their supremely momentary existence. All comparison and allusion, left for the reader to supply, misses the point entirely. And that, of course, *is* the point.

Our train follows a route traveled by mendicant monks, artists, merchant-traders, and such for hundreds of years and made famous by poets and *Ukiyō-e* artists. Under mountains still tipped with snow, rice fields are being prepared for spring planting, tight little rectangles of yellow-green rice shoots nearby the muddy fields farmers till. Dikes are being shored up by field hands in tall black rubber boots and broad straw hats in the drizzle.

Valley after valley, we watch them through the train window. It is hard physical labor, standing with a bent back in muddy fields all day, but surely it is the most dignified, honorable work in the world.

In Japanese, *gohan* means cooked rice. The morning meal is *asagohan;* the noon meal, *hirugohan;* the evening meal, *yugohan. Asa* means morning, *hiru* means noon, and *yu* means evening.

In *A Zen Wave,* Robert Aitken translates the following poem by Bashō:

Furuyu no	The beginning of culture!
hajime ya oku no	Rice-planting songs
ta ue uta	In the innermost part of the country

While he has inverted the second and third lines, he gets the point of it right, despite the error in the first line of his Japanese text—*furuyu* is not a Japanese word; the correct word is *furyu,* "taste" or culture. Aitken's commentary on the poem is excellent.

Rice planting is traditionally "women's work," and the fecundity of the women is associated with the fertility of the soil. In earliest times, this was enhanced by the gifts of the Sun Goddess, Amaterasu Omikami. Tilling, planting, and harvesting were the source not only of the dietary staple, but the root of culture as well.

All day in the fields,
working in mud and water,
bowing to what matters.

We arrive in Sanjo at dusk, greeted by our friend and host, the poet Keida Yusuke. Together, we walk in Hachiman Shrine where the old Zen monk/poet Ryōkan played with village children two centuries ago, a silk ball tucked inside his sleeve.

Four small children see us and stare. Soon, we are all walking together, laughing, playing games, teasing. Tree, my partner, wishes them "good evening" in Japanese, and they all roar with laughter. On the little bridge arching over a pond, we stop and ask to take their picture. They push and pull for position, laughing all the while. They want to know why we're here, and Keida tells them about Ryōkan, then asks the littlest girl, "What are *you* doing here?"

She whispers, "I'm watching a movie!" Keida explains that she's probably never seen a *gaijin* (foreigner) before except in movies.

Secretly, I think the girl and I are the same—two children, one young, one old, seeing one another for the first time, one on a pilgrimage in another country, one a pilgrim at home. Each is delighted with the other, each is thrilled by encounters with the exotic. She glimpses, perhaps, the future; I am engaged with the past. The semi-articulate present provides our perfect present tense—each of us lives a dream.

> "That crazy old monk
> from last year's back again!"
> Children playing in the shrine.
> That old man, Ryōkan,
> thrived on silence, children,
> and a little hot rice wine.

In the outhouse
shivering in a corner
while the storm raged on outside,
Ryōkan, scarcely breathing.
They found him in the morning:
"Shhh! We're playing hide'n'seek!"

Leaving Hachiman Shrine and the children, we walk on alone through quiet, narrow streets along a railroad track. We come to a tiny shrine between two large modern buildings. A small, simple *torii* frames the entrance, and in a few steps we arrive at the back to find a granite stone with Ryōkan's famous "dry leaves" haiku carved in the poet's calligraphy:

Taku hodo wa	Winds blow together
kaze ga motekuru	enough dry leaves here
ochiba kana	to make a fire
	(translation by Keida Yusuke)

At this modest memorial in the midst of town, it is very quiet. Across the street, the grade-school playground is empty. Somewhere unseen, a small bird sings *chiree, chiree*. The sky is gray as stone. A cherry tree blossoms. Several varieties of moss grow among the stones.

Ryōkan lived most of his life alone, much of it in a tiny retreat half up Mount Kugami called Gogo-an, or "Five-Measures-of-Rice Retreat"—named for half a day's ration his predecessor received from Kokujo-ji, the temple farther up the mountain. Here in a town where the poet regularly begged and played, the modesty of this memorial reflects the full modesty of his life.

> That beak-nosed old man
> with his walking stick, a ball
> hidden deep inside his sleeve,
> wandered trails alone.
> "Half-a-*Sho*-of-Rice Retreat."
> In his belly, only a song.

———

What sort of poet
spends so much time with children,
what sort of man goes begging,
lives like a pilgrim
without any destiny?
He sought a way within.

As darkness gradually descends on Sanjo, we walk to Keida's home to settle in and to meet his family. His is a beautiful two-story house with a tiny, impeccably manicured garden in front. The house is the color of light through a shoji screen. Beside the entrance walk, an aging long-needled pine rises through twists and turns almost to the rooftop. A six-foot-high hedge stands between house and sidewalk, muffling noise from the schoolhouse across the street.

Inside, we remove our shoes and carry the heavy pack into an eight-tatami room immediately to our left. The wall facing the street is one long shoji screen with the last daylight softly pouring in. In one corner, a two-foot standing Buddha carved by Keida's father, Seki Kazuo. Behind the Buddha, a scroll with a sutra in a beautiful, albeit unintelligible, hand. To one side, a white vase contains a spray of small white blossoms.

Nothing in this world is as beautifully containing as a thoughtful Japanese room. Paper diffuses light like nothing else. Tatami mats are firm, but soft enough for comfortable kneeling. The painted portions of the walls are a soft sandy green. The simple unpolished grain of the main beam reflects not only the growth of the natural world, but the growth of the human soul as well. A dark table in the center of the room reflects everything that passes by like a pond or lake reflecting winter and summer skies, like rice fields reflecting a thousand moons at night. Such a room carries a great sense of warmth during the long winters of the north, a cool austerity during the swelter of deep summer. Such a room fills one with the elegance of silence, with interior vision composed of shadow, with the awe not of religion, but of the elementally holy.

Keida's wife, Seki Chizuko, his daughter Sanae, and his mother, Seki Kiyo, have prepared a feast in our honor. Everyone is scurrying about the kitchen giggling, laughing, bowing deeply in greeting. Soon the table is spread with sashimi, tempura, pickled vegetables, a delicious nourishing custard called *chawan-mushi,* green tea, and sake. Keida, Tree, and I eat at our table while the women and Mr. Seki either have eaten beforehand or are dining in another room.

We eat and talk and sip sake and eat more, laughing, teasing, savoring both our food and our precious time together.

Afterward, Chizuko joins us. Sanae, she tells us, has prepared her favorite dessert for this occasion, a delicious treat resembling both strawberry ice cream and pudding. It is served cold and melts in the mouth. When Keida teases his daughter, she blushes deeply and laughs and scolds him playfully. She is, like her mother, very beautiful, and has her parents' and grandparents' warm intelligent eyes. All the time we are eating, I am thinking of three generations of women at work in the kitchen, the genuine pleasure they derive from our delight.

> The visitors eat,
> women out in the kitchen
> more present with every bite.

Late in the night, after the food and the wine and the laughter, after Chizuko has rolled out our futons and everyone is asleep, I lie awake in pale light, staring at the ceiling, so overcome with joy I cannot sleep. I would like to rise and slip into the kitchen and cook all night and serve them all in the morning. This soul-work I have called *shadow work,* this labor of love is like no other. It is performed *for its own sake only,* its value measured only by the soul. Such gifts cannot be repaid like debts, but demand nothing in return.

One should remember the basic rule of the tea ceremony: *ichigo-ichie,* the idea that each ceremony, each act of hospitality, is never to be repeated, and thus each service must be fully appreciated and fully attended.

R. H. Blyth quotes an anonymous poem:

Musume no kao wo	Parents eat
futa-oya ga kuu	their daughter's face

and I know the truth of the line, having seen it, unfortunately, too many times. But this is a perfect counterpart: I have filled my belly with woman's love for man; with the love of a wife for her husband and therefore for her husband's friends; I have eaten a mother's love for her son, a daughter's adoration of her father; I have tasted her father's pride and joy in her; I have savored the love of a grown man for his wife, his mother, and his daughter.

Like this room I lie in, the materials are simple. Like the futon which warms my body, it is simply made. Each task, attended to with full attention, made in an act of love, becomes a gift to the world. This gift I have received I shall carry with me wherever my travels lead. And as I go, I, in turn, shall give it away and give it away again, and with each act of giving, the larger and lighter it becomes.

Just before dawn, it begins to drizzle, light rain falling softly on the tile roof. Afraid of disturbing others' sleep, I close my eyes and listen. And I remember a poem Ryōkan wrote in Chinese:

> Sixty years a poor recluse alone
> in a hut near a cliffside shrine.
>
> Night rains fall and carve the cliff.
> On the sill, my candle sputters in the wind.

Ars longa, vita brevis. In its own gentle insistence, the rain punctuates and underscores our temporality. I try to imagine the sound of rain on Ryōkan's thatched roof in the mountains, the sound of rain through bamboo groves, or through the tall cedar forests of my home.

Hearing muffled footsteps outside my door, I rise and dress, leaving Tree to dream. It is Chizuko, already busy with broom and mop, scrubbing the stone floor of the foyer. She gives me a cup of coffee, and I slip out a side door to sit on the stoop in Mrs. Seki's little garden.

Several rows of bonsai nestle among shrubs, trees, and flowers, each as much a garden in its own right as the zen gardens of the temples,—a pebble nestled in moss, a tiny tree twisted carefully horizontally over a planter's edge as though carved by cliffside winds. Studying Mrs. Seki's handiwork, a handiwork passed on through generations, since some of the bonsai are hundreds of years old, I remember several gaijin who complained to me that Japanese art is often "all form and no content." It makes me smile. *Form is the expression of content; content is articulation of form.* The Western mind insists upon a duality which does not in reality exist. The attention to nuance and subtlety, far from minimalizing a work of art, *is* the art of evocation. The insistence upon duality is as useless as trying to "explain" Ryōkan's zen. Alone among the bonsai and the stones and moss of Mrs. Seki's garden, daylight softened by light rain,

I close my eyes in momentary *zazen*, and even in the rainy chill of dawn, sitting in my t-shirt, I am filled with warmth, and feel myself a part, happy enough to cry.

> He wandered trails
> through steep ravines and canyons
> zig-zagging to the summit
> of Mount Yahiko—
> what did he find? A few clouds
> above a vast sea of pine.

We reach Shionori Pass at mid-morning. The mountains are yellow-green with fresh spring growth. A
few strands of mist waft among the trees. How many times
did Ryōkan, begging-bowl in hand, cross between these
mountains in snow, in rain, in summer sunshine?

Just below the summit, off the highway and up a dead-
end road, a single stone with a short poem etched in the
poet's hand. It is strangely quiet—no sound but the dripping of rain through leaves and falling on the memorial
stone. Keida reads us the poem in Japanese. At the foot of
the stone, creeping up its foundation, pale threads of moss
and one tiny chalk-white blossom.

At Izumozaki, on the coast of the Japan Sea, which both
Ryōkan and Bashō visited and wrote about, the weather is
blustery. After nine days of difficult travel, Bashō arrived,
"spirit sore afflicted," as Cid Corman translates the *Oku no
hosomichi,* and wrote:

> rough as the sea is
> reaching over to Sado
> the Heaven's star stream

We visit the largest Ryōkan museum to view his calligraphy. One can clearly see how his hand grew more and more
delicate with age. Here is the silk ball he claimed to have
bounced higher than anyone else—his single instance of
pride. There are several statues of the poet, and several
scrolls in his honor. The building—new, spotlessly clean,
well-lit—seems oddly out of harmony with its subject.
When he was old, the poet begged here frequently. He liked
to climb the hill, as Tree did, to enjoy the view of Sado Island, where exiles were sent for penance. What would he
think of the trinkets, the poor copies of statues and copies
of his calligraphy sold in the busy gift shop at the entrance?

I buy Tree a small kite which says in Ryōkan's hand:

> Above the sky [or "heavens"]
> Great winds

and I think I've never seen four simple characters—each a common radical—say quite as much. At the most simple and obvious level, they are four characters inscribed on a kite; in a more metaphysical vein, they invite a zen interpretation; the poem could pass as a coda for Bashō's vision of the Milky Way over stormy seas along the northwestern coast of Japan.

> He wrote on a kite
> in bold calligraphy,
> *Above Heaven, big winds.*
> Petrels. Shrikes and terns.
> The mountains and waves roll on,
> all singing in the sangha.

We arrive at Mount Kugami in a downpour. The steps winding up to Kokujo-ji are reinforced with small logs. The rain is so heavy, we step gingerly from log to log, each space between containing deep pools of water. The trail winds up through tall long-needled pine, *kiri* or paulownia trees, and dark *hannoki* alder.

The heavy rains tattoo the tin roof of Kokujo-ji and make it sing. The wood is almost white with age. I pause at the *Hondo* to make an offering and a bow, then continue on over the summit and begin the descent to Gogo-an, the stony trail now one long, beautifully rolling waterfall.

> A late spring downpour
> turns the trail to Gogo-an
> into a rushing river.
> Ryōkan's hut is gray
> and dry from years of weather.
>
> Even this rain is an echo.
>
> ———
>
> In a ten-foot hut
> hidden in a forest
> half up Mount Kugami,
> who would come to visit?
> A warbler. A sparrow.
> A song from the kiri trees.

We huddle under the narrow eaves of Gogo-an. While Keida prepares for some photographs, I make my bow to the old man's spirit. Another visitor, a young man of about eighteen, kneels on the veranda with an older man, probably his father. The young man has no arms. His shoes are set neatly beside the door where he has knelt to make his offering. Now his father wants to help him with his shoes, but the young man refuses. His feet are dripping wet, but he manages to get them into his shoes, stands, turns back to face the tiny room with its image of the old monk and a small coin box just inside the door. He bows deeply. His father opens their umbrella, and as they step out into the rain, the young man brushes by me. He nods, smiles faintly, and whispers in English, "Yes."

We drive to Shimazaki to visit the house of Ryōkan's patron, Mr. Kimura, and the grounds where Ryōkan died. Back of the Kimura house a small wooden building houses another museum, this one entirely for his calligraphy. The building creaks as we step in, the ceiling is very low, the light weak.

This, I think, is more suited to the poet. Keida whispers in my ear, "Sabi." *Sabi* comes from the term *sabishi,* meaning "loneliness." It relates to the soul of simple elemental things: the plain wooden beam of a room, a sake or tea cup without ornament, a quality of spiritual depth found only in simplicity. Recently, the term has been applied mostly to the Rikyu-style tea ceremony held in the plainest, least-adorned fashion. But it applies as well to certain kinds of painting and poetry, to pottery and ikebana. It is the expression of a kind of "soul," as Westerners say.

The curator is delivering a lecture to a group of visitors. He carries a long, thin bamboo rod, which he taps against the glass protecting the scrolls or, when exposed, against the scrolls themselves. His voice is strained, and the tap-tap-tap of his bamboo rod is somewhere between annoying and appalling. Keida translates the various scrolls in a whisper while the curator continues his tapping and his lecture, and we leave.

Keida points to the corner of the grounds where the guest house stood before it burned, telling us how difficult it was for Ryōkan in his last days here under the care of a wealthy man. At the main house, an old woman offers us tea, but we thank her and refuse, eager to see Ryusen-ji, the temple up the street which is home to Ryōkan's grave. Along the walkway, Tree points out *veronica* and *companula* and various kinds of moss.

Walking up the street, the rain grows lighter, changing again to a drizzle. And I remember Bashō's student, Hattori Toho, who wrote down his master's advice: "Learn about pine from pine; learn about bamboo from bamboo." Bashō stressed sincerity as the best method for overcoming sub-jectivity, for transcending the separation of self and object. A museum is the most difficult place to learn.

Just inside the torii at the entrance to Ryusen-ji, on a tiny island in the pond, a life-size statue of Ryōkan, broad straw hat and walking stick in his right hand, begging-bowl in his left. He wears a monk's robes with a shawl tied around his shoulders, and straw sandals on his feet. I slip a few coins into his bowl, and we take pictures.

Back behind the temple, on a slight rise, a few graves. Keida leads us to the two in a corner—one is Ryōkan's, the other that of his brother. Another man arrives carrying his infant son. At Ryōkan's grave, he folds his small son's hands in prayer and they bow as one.

The rain has almost stopped. We take a few more photographs and make our bows. The beautiful old temple is absolutely silent. Its shoji screens are patched, the wood worn to smooth ripples. We are soaked to the skin and unspeakably happy and filled with an inner lightness. We stop at the hondo to make a last bow and a small donation before turning back to the road. Just above the fence, a single cherry branch is blooming, and children shout and laugh somewhere far in the distance.

> Ryusen-ji—two graves
> for Ryōkan and his brother.
> A heavy mist shrouds the world,
> wrapping things in dream.
> Birth-death cycle?—All the same:
> cherry blossoms float downstream.

Keida's father, Seki Kazuo, is carving ten thousand Buddhas. The earliest were large, like the two-foot Buddha in "our" room. But the thousands of later ones are tiny, only two or three inches each. Old Mr. Seki, retired from city offices, rises each morning to greet the day with a reading from the *Han-nya-shin-gyo*, the *prajna-paramita sutra*. Sitting out in Mrs. Seki's garden again, I hear his voice faintly as he recites, soft and warm, the music of the ages. Next week, he will turn seventy-seven. Nine thousand and several hundred Buddhas have been completed. The sutra over, he comes out of his room, delighted to find me up. We sit quietly while his wife and Chizuko set the table with rice and miso soup, pickled vegetables, and boiled eggs. Soon, Sanae, Tree, and Keida join us and we eat, chatter, and laugh.

After the table is cleared, we ask to see Mr. Seki's carving tools. He brings out a small wooden box and opens it gingerly. Inside are four small carpenter's chisels, each razor sharp. There are also several small blocks of wood which will soon become new images. On the back of each carving of Kannon, bodhisattva of compassion, Mr. Seki writes the *Enmei-jukku-Kannon-kyo*, or *Long Life Ten Phrases Sutra*. There is no need to ask why he has undertaken this enormous task. The answer was given in his sutra. Each image is informed by a deep reverent humility and a quiet joy. While he talks, Mrs. Seki kneels beside him, smiling contentedly.

Mr. Seki tells us about a Buddha he carved which is now housed in the cloistered innermost sanctum at a temple of Kannon. He goes back into his room and returns with a scroll which he unrolls. It is a rubbing from the accompanying stone in Kawabata Yasunari's hand. On the back, he has copied the story from the newspapers which gives the details of the stone and Buddha—all the evidence of their labors since neither stone nor Buddha carries an attribution. In his voice and gestures there is a far greater sense of honor than of pride.

"This body," Hakuin Zenji sang, "is the body of the Buddha." Every Buddha is a wooden-head.

We board the little train, on our way to Kamishio where Keida-*sensei* (honorable teacher) teaches eighth-grade English. Chizuko stands in the station waving and waving until we can no longer see her, the train chugging along through bright sunlit levees where field hands are repairing dikes and beginning to plant new rice shoots. A hawk circles the foothills, and far beyond we see Mount Sumon still capped with snow.

Twenty minutes later, we arrive at our station and climb into a cab—it is a holiday and there are no buses for the forty-minute ride through Tochio and up into the hills. And all the while, rice fields, one after another, some with herons, some with gulls, the rice shoots almost yellow, the water sparkling clear.

As we ride, I tell Keida Bashō's poem about rice fields as the source of culture. He explains that we are traveling through a part of Japan in which rice fields are most plentiful. All this chatter about rice fields and Bashō—I'm certain the driver thinks we're crazy. And I remember how Ryōkan signed his name—*Dai-gu*, or "Great Fool" Ryōkan.

> No *kensho,* no insight,
> nothing mirrored in the levees
> but the vast blue empty sky.

Kamishio

Kamishio is a village on the outskirts of Tochio, nestled at the intersection of three valleys. To the east, a low range of tree-covered mountains. To the south, two valleys are separated by more hills, Mount Sumon snow-capped in the distance as though painted on the sky. To the west, mountains rise more abruptly, the hills darker. To the north, a broad valley of levees with narrow lanes leading to small clusters of homes.

We arrive in the late afternoon, the sun settling over the hills, pale yellow light dancing on rice fields and casting the shadows of workers a long way over the water. A few tractors moving almost imperceptibly. Here and there, people in broad straw hats shovel dirt along the dikes.

Keida's cottage lies at the end of a narrow lane, rice fields on either side. Beyond the cottage, a few old hannoki alder are just beginning to bud, and beyond the alder, a river, unseen, gently sings. And just beyond the river, thick forests cover a sharp ridge.

Here, Keida-sensei makes his home from early Monday morning through Friday night, living in two small rooms. One, a kitchen, faces east. The other, a bare eight-tatami room with shoji covering the windows, serves as bedroom, study, library, and whatever else a teaching poet may need.

It is normal for a teacher to be moved from one school to another every few years. Consequently, Keida sees his family only once a week. For five-and-a-half days, he is teacher and vice principal in Kamishio, living alone in a tiny cottage among the levees. On Saturday afternoon, when classes end, he takes the bus to Mitsuke, then a train to Sanjo City, only to return to Kamishio long before dawn on Monday mornings. This arrangement must place an enormous burden on a family. For the past fifteen years, I've spent half or more of each year living in motels, teaching in prisons, public schools, and universities, so I can imagine the sense of isolation; I know all too well the longing for one's children and friends and community.

Late Sunday afternoon, the village is almost silent. A few birds chirp in trees down along the river. Shadows grow long, and the old wooden houses, snuggled under broad eaves, are dark, taking on a dusky brown color the shade of miso soup. Walking the lane toward the village market, I think this valley exists almost beyond time, the only real evidence of the twentieth century, now that the tractors are gone, are the few telephone and electric lines running along the road—a single grim reminder that Japan's electricity is almost entirely nuclear-generated.

I think of the old recluse-poets Saigyō, Chomei, and Ikkyū who chose to simplify their lives by rejecting material convenience. Each would like this village with its fertile fields surrounded by forests, mountains, rivers, and streams. It is indeed *ukiyo*—a floating world, reminding me of a poem by Ryōkan, translated by Burton Watson:

> Water to draw
> brushwood to cut
> greens to pick—
> all in moments when
> morning showers let up.

But it is evening. We're to market for our dinner. Across the tiered levees, in the lengthening shadows of mountains, ten thousand frogs begin to sing.

The old schoolhouse stands on a small rise at the beginning of foothills, an aging two-story building, its wood now deep brown from years of exposure to harsh winter weather. We take a snapshot from the bare schoolground, then Keida unlocks the door and we go in. We remove our shoes and he gives us "visitor's slippers" and leads us on our tour. But for the Japanese language, it could be a rickety old school in Browning, Montana, or Parawan, Utah, or any of a hundred village schools I've visited over the years. There are the same science classrooms with deep-sinks and with charts tacked on the walls, but written in Japanese; the same history and language and geography classes; the same rolled maps and old, chalky blackboards. But there are also bare wires and extension cords schools in the U.S. would never permit. The floor creaks loudly as we walk.

Keida tells us that soon the school will be closed and torn down; there are new schools being built nearby. I think of all the students who struggled in these rooms and halls, some now laboring in the fields, others gone to cities far away. A good school is a kind of temple where one comes, if lucky, to find oneself alone, where one should begin to glimpse one's own deepest inner nature and begin to become a citizen of the world.

There are two dominant phenomena in a decent school: 1) somewhere amidst the chaos, there is order; and 2) one never comprehends its meaning until long after it is over. Like a museum, a school is necessary, but a terrible place to learn.

Walking on complaining floors through empty rooms, the closing lines of a wonderful poem by W. S. Merwin come back again:

> Please teach me
> I am almost ready to learn

Yugen. We in the West associate the term with ink paintings of misty landscapes, steeply rising wooded peaks, and far below, a pilgrim crossing a rickety bridge, his small satchel tied to a walking stick. *Yugen*. The expression of "other-wordliness" in poetry or painting. The term, borrowed from early Chinese Buddhism where it was used to express the "depth of meaning" in the Dharma-teaching, was introduced as a literary term in Japan by Mibu no Tadamine, co-compiler of the *Kokinshu* in the tenth century.

In his twelfth-century commentary on poetics, the *Mumyosho,* Kamo no Chomei says he does not understand the term completely, then goes on to say that it is related to *yojo*—an atmosphere created not by what is clearly stated in the words themselves, but by what is revealed naturally. "On an autumn evening, for example, there is no color in the sky, nor any sound, and although we cannot give a definite reason for it, we are somehow moved to tears."

And later still, Zen and Noh used the term to mean "ghostly qualities," and it came to be an important term in ink painting.

In this valley where shadows merge with shadows, the evening merges one thing with another—mountain shadows, mountains, soaking rice fields, the dark empty sky without moon or stars—everything interpenetrating, merging in mutual reflection suggesting deeper mystery.

Here, far from the noisy, distracting busyness of Tokyo, one comes into the realm of the real world. The Chinese *Mo-ho Chih-kuan* translates two interconnected Sanskrit terms: *samatha,* or "motionlessness," and *vipasyana,* or "contemplation." In Japanese, it is called *shikan.* It is a meditative state in which the mind enters a state of perception utterly free of discrimination between mind and matter, self and object, where the only permanence is impermanence, and change—whether subtle or violent—remains the essence of being.

Those frogs singing in hundreds of fields are only frogs. They are not a symbol. The shadows on the water are shadows; the water, water. It is evening in Sanjo, where Mr. Seki has put away his simple chisels in their small brown wooden box; evening in Tokyo where almost no one notices any light beyond the neon and noise; evening in the bamboo forests along the shores of Lake Biwa near Kyoto where Ikkyū contemplated suicide; it is nightfall on Sunset Hill where Ryōkan and Bashō sat waiting patiently for the moon, Sado Island floating on the horizon like a dream. A few night-sounds, a wealth of silence.

We eat and talk until it grows late, then lay out the futons and sleep. And I dream of Bashō's famous frog leaping into the sound of water. I dream of Mr. Seki reciting his morning sutra and taking out his tools.

Ten Thousand Buddhas
for Seki Kazuo

The first pale light
silhouettes the mountains.

All along the valley's rising hills,
deep woods of gray hannoki alder

begin to bud, a few crows
clucking in their branches.

Beyond the trees,
the river sings.

Countless shallow pools
reflect the empty morning sky

where, last night,
thousands of moons were shining.

Somewhere, a farm wife
begins her family's breakfast.

Men who work the stone-crushing plant
rise, pull on overalls, yawn,

and greet the day.
The world is difficult, but good.

From the woods, a faint *bu-pō-so,*
bu-pō-so, song of the Buddha-bird.

And once again,
the frogs begin their sutra.

———

That's not Mount Sumeru, snowy cold,
defining the horizon. These forests

are no man's *arana*—groves
of a yogin's retreat.

Pitched against this sky, Mount Sumon
towers over valleys

children call Mole and Wasabi,
over mirrored rice fields,

rising like a dream, like a phantom,
like any mountain seen

by a man with a broken begging-bowl
two hundred years ago

or five hundred years before that:
Ryōkan or Kamo no Chomei

might live there in a hut;
Bashō might wear it like a hat.

What's any mountain but a signpost
along a wanderer's route?

A thousand fields in a thousand valleys
like the thousand arms of Kannon.

Ten thousand mountains over ten thousand fields
with rice shoots to be planted—

the dew of the world, the bent back.
The fields soak. The soil is rich black.

In the hour before dawn, pale clouds drift down from the north, painting the eastern hills a soft sumi gray. It is the quiet hour. After zazen in the kitchen, I make a cup of coffee and sit at the window watching light break over the eastern hills, the first morning sound the *clack, clack* of a crow from somewhere down by the river. The clouds slowly turn and roll. The cloud patterns recall a poem by Bashō:

Hana no kumo	A cloud of flowers,
kane wa Ueno ka	a temple bell. Ueno?
Asakusa ka	Is it Asakusa?

In his commentary on this poem, Robert Aitken points out that Bashō, sitting under the cherry blossoms, has entered the "undifferentiated aesthetic continuum," and achieved the consciousness of a "divine fool."

Kamo no Mabuchi says in his eighteenth-century *Kaiko*, "The emotion in one's heart produces the voice of poetry." It is a common sentiment, echoing the famous preface to the *Kokinshu* which states simply, "Poetry begins in the heart." But what is the emotion producing the voice of Bashō's poem, a poem which is almost silent? *Mushin.* The *mu* is "emptiness" or "nothingness," but not to be confused with existential nothingness. It is the "emptiness" of the *Lotus Sutra,* the Sanskrit *sunyata* which is complete, utter inter-co-dependence. *Mu* is beautiful nothingness, *mu* is what is left when illusion is stripped away from all phenomena.

And *shin?* It is the heart/mind—not two things joined, but one thing which we often pretend is two, but which, try as we might, we cannot separate.

Show me your own original face before your parents were born. *Mu!* What is it at the center of the heart/mind? *Mu!* Do cows have Buddha-nature? Such joy in foolishness! Such silliness at the heart of the most serious discussion of philosophy.

I sit, listening to crows. They are full of serious shenanigans and earnest mischief like renegade monks swooping around in shiny black robes in the forest.

In Japanese, the crow is called *karasu*. Most are jungle crows called *hashibuto-karasu,* or carrion crows, *hashiboso-karasu*. In pronunciation, the final *u* is virtually silent, so that it sounds like *ka-ross, ka-ross,* their name being onomatopoeic. The jungle crow is slightly larger, has a thicker, more curved bill, and a very pronounced forehead. But only hearing them, how to distinguish one from the other? Have you heard the temple bells at Ueno?

Down along the river, several crows have gathered, and they call back and forth in their own enlightened mocking, *Karasu! Karasu! Karasu!*

The clouds look like huge heavenly branches of cherry blossoms—*kumo no hana*—flowers of cloud. For only a moment, sunlight bursts between the mountaintops and the low clouds, then vanishes. The morning temple bells of Asakusa ring in the huge megalopolis of Tokyo. It has been 299 years since Bashō wandered these north country roads. Even Bashō tried desperately to give up poetry in order to embrace the grand silence of *mushin,* but try as he might, the poetry spoke again.

Samuel Beckett, awarded the Nobel Prize in literature, had no comment. After days or weeks holed up in his room, he was finally persuaded to appear for a photograph. Still he had no comment. Eventually, an old friend persuaded him, "Please Mr. Beckett, just a comment on receiving the Nobel Prize."

"Every word," Sam Beckett replied, "is an unnecessary stain on silence and nothingness."

Mushin, Sam Beckett, crown prince of the comedy of zen.

> Even daybreak,
> such a momentary thing.
> What is it in the heart?
> With no word to explain it,
> something sings.

In the tiny Kamishio market, we buy the large white noodles called *udon,* some tofu, spinach, an egg, a few small dried herring, and a package of broth for the base. The man who runs the market is worried for us. "Do the *gaijin,*" he asks Keida, "know how to make udon?"

"Yes," Keida assures him, "the *gaijin* do know how to boil noodles and spinach."

While Keida is fulfilling duties at school, we cook our lunch and eat. The udon is delicious despite being loaded with MSG. Eating, I remember the Buddhist terms *jo, ju, e,* and *ku*—formation, persistence, destruction, and return to emptiness. A simple lunch of udon explains the idea perfectly. Just as they represent a biological reality, these terms also explain the development of the poem: it begins to take form with the rhythm of emotion in the heart; through the persistence of a poet's dedication to craft and knowledge, it becomes a defined thing in its own right; through the act of making the gift—the poem—and giving it, the poet destroys the original need to speak, and once again enters a state of emptiness within. And it is true also of learning. Otherwise, it would not be imperative that we "unlearn" so much of what transpires between teacher and student, whether in the classroom or in the *zendo.*

Biological reality, spiritual growth, the birth of culture planted in rice seedlings, the truth and force of poetry—it's all right here in heavy white noodles—the whole of history, our present international despair, our triumphs and our glories, the future we all fear—it's here in the noodles we slurp, it's here in steamy broth we drink, so good, so simple and essential, so miraculous going down.

Kamishio Chugakko could be any middle school in Small Town, U.S.A. Before English class begins, we have a cup of green tea with Keida-sensei. The hallways boom with the busyness of adolescents, with shouts and laughter and teasing. At the bell, we climb the stairs to our classroom, and all the way along we hear the boisterousness of young men and women. But as Keida-sensei opens the classroom door, silence falls like a stone. Everyone stands at attention. "Good morning," he says in English.

"Good morning," everyone says in unison.

The students are very curious about the *gaijin,* but painfully shy. Keida-sensei has a little difficulty getting the students to ask questions. Some try to hide behind their classmates, other look like they are struggling to vanish into their wooden seats. Several of the girls appear as if they will burst into tears when they are called upon to speak. They are in the eighth grade, in their first of five years of English. We try to answer each question, speaking slowly and only in the present tense. Yes, we like Japanese cooking; yes, we enjoy sleeping on a futon; yes, we think Kamishio is very beautiful and an interesting place to visit. We tell them where we come from and what we do. We talk about Japanese poetry. They struggle and they blush deeply and some get tears in their eyes. But they are kind and curious and polite. And at the end of class, they sing us their school song, relieved to be singing Japanese.

Afterward, we stop downstairs for a cup of coffee with the principal. While we are waiting for him, there is a buzz at the door—fifteen or twenty girls have gathered to see the *gaijin,* to say "Thank you," and to ask whether it would be okay to shake hands. Tree and I shake hands with each in turn, telling them, "Thank you," and "Nice to meet you."

We chat with the principal, finish our coffee, and leave. As we cross the schoolyard, many of the students shout *"Harro!"* and wave. We wave back. Walking back down the road, tears well up in my eyes.

On the *shinkansen* back to Tokyo, we cross the tiered valleys of rice fields once again. We wind through beautiful mountains. As darkness falls, I notice a girl of about eighteen in the seat in front of us. She watches us in the mirror the window has become. She sometimes peers at us from around the corner of the seat. Her fascination with the *gaijin* lasts more than an hour, until we are entering Tokyo, but she doesn't speak. Tree holds up the book she is reading so the girl can see that it's Ryōkan. At the first Tokyo stop, the girl stands and pulls her bag from the overhead rack, then turns to us and says, "Would you like a stamp?" and hands us each a pair of stamps, one a memorial *Oku no hosomichi,* the other a sleepy-looking dragon.

We thank her, and she leaves. We are heartbroken that we didn't have some small thing we could have given in return, saddened that we didn't speak to her sooner. Just a pretty young woman, curious about another country, wanting to practice her English with travelers on a bullet train.

> A girl's timid eyes and smile—
> sealed away forever like a sacred stamp
> locked in the book of the heart.

Little Song for John Solt
after a lecture on how contemporary Japanese
poets came to reject the tanka

This is Japan, where,
to the horror of some friends,
I'm writing waka.

———

But there is no poem.
There is no paper, no pen.
A silence listens.

———

In Ogikubo,
it is dawn, and turtle doves
sound like making love.

———

Here, alone, breathing,
the mind is an empty sky—
no moon, no heaven.

———

Sabi—aloneness—
the warmth of a well-made cup.
Drink from this water.

———

A magpie explores
the avenues of the tree.
How softly wind blows!

———

Like water, like sky,
the breath of the mind uncoils.
The text is empty.

———

What did Hui Neng say?
If you don't know the answer,
why ask the question.

―――

Take this cup from me.
Drinking, you soon grow thirsty.
The cup is empty.

―――

A magpie, a dove,
a tree against the blank sky.
The heart is a sponge.

―――

Flesh and bone and blood
are only the moment's dream.
Still, they are enough.

―――

Here is the poem.
The text remains unwritten.
No thing's what it seems.

Asakusa Kannon

At Asakusa, there is a huge temple of Kannon. Its official name is Sensoji, but everyone calls it simply Asakusa Kannon. The temple was founded after two brothers caught a tiny wooden statue of Kannon while fishing in the nearby Sumida River in 628. One of the brothers recognized the image as that of Avalokitesvara, or Kannon, and had the image enshrined. Twenty years later, the priest Shokai had the Kannon-do, or main hall, built. Seeing the statue as a revelation, he had it sealed away from human eyes and placed within the innermost sanctuary. The statue itself is of the same kind carved by Seki Kazuo, only two or three inches in height.

In the tiny fishing village of Asakusa, the great temple became a landmark. Another priest, the temple's co-founder, Jikaku, carved a statue exactly like the original one for people to see.

During the Kamakura period nearly five hundred years later, the temple was expanded and enlarged, thanks to the patronage of the shogunate. In 1387, the temple's huge bronze bell was cast and installed near the garden pond. It is the oldest of its kind in Tokyo. During the Edo period, Sensoji became the cultural center of what would still later become known as the Meiji Restoration and the birth of modern Tokyo.

Sensoji Hondo, the main sanctuary hall, was destroyed during the fire-bombing of Tokyo on March 10, 1945. Rebuilding was completed in October of 1958. It is assumed that the figure of Kannon, sealed away, survived. Presently, the temple supports a hospital, schools, a social welfare center, and innumerable other activities.

Meanwhile, the figure of Kannon has remained hidden from human eyes for thirteen hundred years. In the Hondo, the Goku-den, or altar, is gold-leafed, and highly ornate. To the right side, a Fudō-dō, or shrine to the God of Justice, Fudō, a figure seen most often amidst flames and with sword raised. To the other side, the Aizen-dō, a shrine to the God of Love.

> At Asakusa,
> Kannon, thirteen centuries hidden—
> Between Love and Justice.

On my second visit to Asakusa Kannon, I arrive at the Hondo just as the monks are beginning a recitation of *Moho Renge Kyo,* the *Lotus Sutra.* The grounds are thick with people despite steady June rain. I toss a few coins into the collection box, place my palms together and bow, then move off to one side for a little standing meditation while tourists and mendicants, one by two, complete their various businesses before the altar. The chant of the sutra is steady, a low rolling rhythm. I close my eyes. And I remember my one experience with *rohatsu,* a week-long intensive meditation practice the first week of December.

Twenty-five years before, while I was on Okinawa as a U.S. Marine, I began the practice of *zazen.* I was encouraged in this practice by my friend, Eizo, an old man who worked shining shoes, polishing brass, and washing clothes for the officers in the Bachelor Officers' Quarters. I had arranged a leave, and for another G.I. to cover for me at the motor pool office where I worked. Eizo took me to a small temple in Naha for rohatsu, where I experienced pain and elation like none I had ever before known.

For five days and nights, I participated, feeling dim-witted, slow, pain in my knees like they were made of broken glass. The whole week, rain poured down and winds blasted trees and whined under the broad eaves of the meditation hall. The *jikijitsu,* the monk who leads the practice, grew particularly fond of whacking my shoulders with the stick. But the pain of the stick was small compared to my self-consciousness. It was 1961, and Okinawa had been occupied by U.S. forces for nearly twenty years, the whole island being turned into one huge military base. With my nearly shaved head, I might as well have been in uniform. With every whack of the stick, however, I renewed my pledge to see rohatsu through to the end. I didn't understand the sutra. Eizo said it didn't matter. I made no progress with my koan. Eizo said any response was a response and not to worry. My legs ached until I could barely stand for *kinhin,* or walking meditation. During breaks, Eizo massaged my knees.

A quarter of a century later, hair cut almost as short as it was then, but with a gray beard, I stand inside Sensoji listening to the *Lotus Sutra.* A monk begins the part where the chant is joined by the drum, and I can feel the rhythms building somewhere in my bones. People hurry in and out, the rain continuing to spatter loudly just beyond the open veranda.

And I think of Eizo, by now dead. I remember the young Marine wanting to learn zazen, a young man lonely and filled with self-doubt who fell in love with an old man and then with the old man's beautiful grand-daughter. Now middle-aged, my beard gray and face lined with years, I think of the ravaged face of Eizo, a stooped, poverty-stricken saint on the island of Okinawa. Drum and sutra continue to build their interlocking syncopation.

And I remember Eizo's grand-daughter's face the rainy night she refused my hand in marriage. I remember weeping in the zendo at rohatsu, whether from physical pain or from rejection—perhaps both.

Suddenly, but very quietly, the sutra concludes. I open my eyes. The temple, completely rebuilt in the 1950s, seems as ancient as the figure fished from the Sumida River hundreds of years ago. I pick up my umbrella and go back out into the rain. But I can't keep from laughing out loud with a mixture of joy and relief, and I can't keep those same sad tears from falling.

Rin-no-ji, Nikko

High in the mountains west of Tokyo, a cluster of temples and a Shinto shrine nestle among sixteen thousand huge cryptomeria trees planted under the direction of the Tokugawa shogun Iyeyasu. But the temple itself, Rin-no-ji, was founded long before that.

In 766, during the height of the Nara period, Shodo-shonin, a Tendai Buddhist high priest with a deep faith in the virtues of Kannon, crossed the Daiya River to climb the steep mountain and there establish a hermitage, Shihon-ryu-ji, far from the bustling capital. In 784, Shodo-shonin climbed still deeper into the mountains, crossed behind Kegon Falls along the Ojiri River, which flows from a huge lake, and there established Chuzen-ji, "Middle Zen Temple," with its primary image of Tachiki, or "Standing-tree" Kannon, which the priest carved himself from a Judas-tree.

During the Heian period, another priest, Kobo-daishi (better known as Kukai), visited the hermitage at Rin-no-ji and was so moved by his experience that he established several smaller temples. Kukai was, in turn, followed by another high priest, Jikaku-daishi, who built the great San-butsudō, or "Three Buddhas Temple," and installed the "Three Divine Manifestations in Nikko," figures of Bato, or "Horse-headed" Kannon, Amida Buddha, and Kannon-of-a-Thousand-Arms, called Senju Kannon.

During the Kamakura period, these temples prospered under the patronage of successive lords of the Genji clan. And still later, during the Tokugawa period when Bashō lived, the fifty-third Abbot, Jigen-daishi, built a Shinto mausoleum to house the ashes of the first Tokugawa shogun, Iyeyasu, who had been a patron. The shogun's grandson, Iemitsu, employed fifteen thousand workers over twenty years to construct the Toshogu Shrine.

Among the various temples, there is a five-story pagoda, and a fifty-foot Sorinto pillar containing a thousand volumes of sutras and symbolizing world peace. The mixture of Chinese and Japanese styles sometimes contrasts sharply, sometimes with subtlety. Yomeimon, or "Sunset Gate" is surely one of the most elaborate entrances in the world. But even Sunset Gate pales in comparison to Karamon Gate's four-gabled and heavily and ornately inlayed edifice with its engravings of Chinese sages.

The Nikko complex also boasts the three most famous monkeys in the world. They demonstrate the three major principles of the Tendai Sect: "See no evil; speak no evil; hear no evil." Copies of the original carving are offered for sale in every knick-knack shop and curio counter in the town of Nikko below. And I wonder what Shodo-shonin would say about the booths peddling pseudo-Buddhist ticky-tacky to the tourists, what he would say about the ornate gates and buildings constructed around his simple mountain hermitage over the past twelve hundred years.

Walking among these beautiful old buildings, listening to tourists "oooh" and "aaah," my mind returns time and again to my own center of meditation—a simple wooden platform set among stones with additional stones placed on three of its four corners by my daughter years ago—Moon Watching Pavilion. It sits at the back of our garden among alder and cedar trees. No roof. No walls. There are no images of the Buddha, no votive tablets, no sutras—nothing but a simple wooden platform two feet above the muddy soil with simple stepping-stones leading the way in. And for the first time in months, I long for an hour of zazen alone in the afternoon sunshine or, better yet, in the evening as the moon rises through the trees.

Bashō, wandering these mountains on his pilgrimage three hundred years ago, described the Urami-no-taki, or "Seen-from-Behind Waterfall," near Chuzen-ji, in detail. But it was Nikko more than any other place which touched him most deeply: he called it "the most sacred of all shrines."

> Under giant cryptomeria,
> staggered by a thousand years of labors,
> I long for a little *yaza,*—
> silent meditation of the night.

Resting near the huge stone torii, I hear a bird calling *ju-jun! ju-jun!* and look up—*seguro-sekirei,* the Japanese wagtail, perches on a limb fifteen feet overhead. With a white stripe over the eye and a white patch under the chin, its head otherwise entirely black, it looks like a village priest with white hair and white goatee in a frock of black, only the white belly and wingtips to suggest vestigial under-robes. *Ju-jun, ju-jun!* and the little wagtail flies away.

Down the broad trail below, canvas-covered stands sell snacks and beverages, giving the whole entrance way to Toshogu Shrine a carnival-like atmosphere. Off to one side, a dozen cab drivers stand around in small groups smoking and chatting while their fares tour the shrine. Under the cryptomeria, an underbrush rather like salal—viney and tangled, leaves thick and waxy. But none of the cabbies can tell me its name.

Back down the mountain and into town for the train. We walk around looking at displays of sweets and trinkets but can't find a good *bento* (lunchbox) or *sushiya.* I buy *sashimi* in a tiny store. It begins to rain. Fishermen stand in their high boots casting down the Daiya, probably fishing for trout. Mist descends on the mountains, rolling into the canyons.

Two Songs for Tanabata Matsuri

1. Altair and Vega

Spring has gone. The brief hour
of cherry blossom time
has passed again into the heart's mind
which revises and refines
the momentary loves
which last longer than a lifetime.

Spring has gone again,
and once again, *kumo no umi*—
a sea of clouds
darken the rainy season.
The paper sags
on the shoji screens.

Even inside the house,
washed clothes won't dry,
books begin to mildew,
the bed feels damp all night.
Then comes July,
a swelter, a stifling light.

But it is Seven/Seven,
Altair and Vega meet again
high above the Yangtze.
Once each year the Cowboy, *Kengyu,*
returns to his lover,
Shokujo, the Weaving Girl.

In the topography of the heart
it is the hour of vistas,
it is the hour of seeing deeply

into the warm night's core:
what happens here now
has happened ten billion times before.

What is a river
between two lovers, what is a sea
to cross, what is the Milky Way
but a river of stars
pouring down from heaven?
Come here, beside me.

That love which seeks love
is only a human affection.
Stars drift and shine and intertwine
only in our eyes.
Being itself becomes a metaphor.
"Meaning" has no meaning.

Altair and Vega, Kengyu and Shokujo,—
the story of love divided
is the story of every love.
The end of the story
is neither happy nor tragic.
Like Altair and Vega,

we ride the night sky alone,
reflecting only the light
which shines on us
from other burning stars.
Be still. Stay a moment
just as you are.

It is the seventh day
of the seventh month—
the mundane world

lies millions of miles away.
Let me undress you slowly
by the light of the Milky Way.

We burst into flame,
burning through the night.
It is a dream of water,
of galaxies in flight,
it is the story of the Phoenix,
it is a sea of dream, an ocean of delight.

Let me kiss your mouth
and breathe the scent of your hair.
I love you cautiously, slowly, deeply,
like a river under the stars,
like a river
reflecting Vega and Altair.

2. Sweating It Out
        after Tanabata Festival,
        written in the margins
        of the Man'yoshu

There is nothing elegant
about sweat.
                The gray dawn breaks
over Musashino Plain
and a few small raindrops fall.
The dust is not stirred,
                        the birds
are almost silent: sparrow-
chirps, but no doves, no magpies.
Even the crows grow silent
in this swelter.

At my desk,
sitting in my shorts, shirtless,
ten minutes from the shower,
skin clings to skin, a thick glaze
coating the body.
          Here I sit,
reading Prince Aki's *choka*
in the *Man'yoshu,* wasting
my life on poetry, dreams
of spring rain,
          the tormented
songs of a people spoken
in a voice at once human
and humane. Prince Aki
loved a woman
          he was not
supposed to love, a woman
forbidden, one far beneath
his station. Separated
by Imperial
          command,
he longed for clouds and rain, for
the wings of a bird to fly, for
a few gentle words to speak

a plainly elegant truth.

———

A few perspiration drops
stain the page as I read. Twelve
hundred years have vanished in
a single moment.
          The stars
called Cowboy and Weaving Girl

meet high over the River
of Heaven, crossing a bridge
of magpies.
　　　　Tanabata
Matsuri passes without
a poem, the streamers hung
in the city streets are made
of plastic,
　　　　and the lovers
who stood on the bridge and dreamed
of arms outstretched for pillows
have vanished in the water.
No moon.
　　　　Only the swelter
of Yamato in July,
only the same ageless dream
of crossing Heaven's River.
What does it mean,
　　　　　　this old song
of love and sorrow? The years
have not changed. We have not changed
ourselves. We also love dreams
of dreaming,
　　　　a lover's song
of parting and denial,
of hope in deep affection.
The heart's music has not changed
in a thousand
　　　　thousand years.
And still, there is no meaning.
Here, sweating over a song
a thousand years old, I come
into myself.

Being is enough.

       To love
is plenty. The past is not
over, it is becoming.

   Envoy

A new year begins.
Every morning this morning.
Every day begins today.
Another year passed.
Sunlight. Clouds. Birds on the wing.
Only this moment. At last.

Sitting Zen, Working Zen, Feminist Zen

When the Third Patriarch of Zen, Sengtsan, was still a student of the Second Patriarch, Hui-k'o, he went to his Master and said, "I am diseased; please cleanse me of my sin."

Hui-k'o said, "Bring me your sin and I will cleanse you of it."

Sengtsan thought a long time. "I cannot get at it."

"Then I have cleansed you of it."

This story and many others from R. H. Blyth's *Zen and Zen Classics* filled my days aboard a troop ship bound for Yokohama more than a quarter-century ago. Eighteen years old, I had squandered my adolescence in and out of jails until a judge suggested I "seek discipline in the service of the U.S. Marine Corps or spend a like amount of time in the custody of the state." I had read a little about Zen Buddhism, mostly things suggested by Kenneth Rexroth. As I would slowly discover over the following decades, Zen means sitting. But I will always be grateful to R. H. Blyth for his little books of commentary and translation, and I continue to read them for the sheer intelligence of the prose.

While stationed on Okinawa, reading Blyth, Suzuki, and others, I learned to sit *zazen*. I visited temples and attended lectures. I sat almost daily, my military schedule permitting, but only for very short periods—fifteen or twenty minutes per day. I extended my stay there to pursue my studies. More than a quarter-century has passed since those two years concluded, but my practice remains relatively unchanged. Out of this early practice, I adopted a standard of nonviolence, the position of the Conscientious Objector, a view I hold to this day.

Hui Neng, the Sixth Patriarch, says we sit zazen not in order to become enlightened, but because we *are* enlightened. In his extraordinary little volume of "Essays in Zen Buddhist Ethics," *The Mind of Clover,* Robert Aitken devotes a brief piece to the term *samu,* a term D. T. Suzuki translates unsatisfactorily as "labor." As Aitken points out, *sa* means "production—tillage or harvest"; *mu* means "to devote attention." Thus, we remember the words of Pai-chang, "A day of no samu is a day of no eating." Pai-chang's words work in two directions at once. "No work, no food," is barely adequate to his insight. He also means that we are nourished by our devotion and attention to labors.

At a time when all emphasis was being placed on zazen, the Rinzai monk Hakuin went around Soto meditation halls and poked the monks, "Get up and go do something useful, the work is part of the koan!"

And that is the story. Whether we call it by its Chinese name, *tso-ch'an,* or whether we know it from the Japanese *zazen,* we cannot know it without *doing* it. Talking about sitting is not sitting. In order to comprehend attentive inaction, one must begin with contemplation. Dialogue won't help. I do not sit in order to "become enlightened." Millions of people have died at the hands of those who professed to seek enlightenment. I sit in order to sit. If Hui Neng believes my sitting is evidence of enlightenment, he may also wish to account for my shortcomings—call them my "endarkenments."

The other side of sitting is *samu*. Not simply working, but investing in devoted labors. There are plenty of monks raking sand in elegant temple gardens in Japan who never really see the sand they rake. There are some who think the sand is only a metaphor, some who think it a legend or a fable, a symbol, a tradition. Perhaps there are even some who believe Zen can enter the heart through the eye.

Raking the sand, there is plenty of sand to be raked, and indeed some of it seems at first to be the sands of one's own life, sands of the hourglass, or sands from a remembered beach. *Samu* suggests a right-mindfulness toward one's work, toward *all* of one's work. Raking the sand, one sifts through illusions and deceits, through guilt and embarrassment and anger, until, eventually, slowly and carefully raking the sand, one gets at last to the sand.

The work is part of the koan.

Action is measured by inaction, inaction informs action—the Tao of zazen. Zen discipline comes down to this—attentiveness; doing and not-doing; being. As with poetry, insights attainable through the practice of zazen arise out of attention to detail, to daily moment-by-moment attention to detail.

Americans often get caught up in the notion of highest perfect enlightenment. We live in a culture which has invested heavily in lies promoting the idea of immediate self-gratification. Caught between our illusion of prosperity and the hard reality of homelessness, poverty, despair, and murderous foreign relations, we often try desperately *not* to see. Sometimes this is accomplished by turning over our own individual responsibility to "faith," to religion. Some even attempt to escape into Zen. But Zen is not an evasion of personal accountability.

Some zennists believe in sudden complete realization;

some believe in gradual clarification. Some follow teaching which emphasizes koan study; some emphasize recitation of the sutras. What are we to say when each claims the one Way to Nirvana?

I have never been to Nirvana and I don't know anyone there. In *this* world, Samsara, the cycle-of-birth-and-death, I am witness to the innumerable births and deaths of each inevitable day. Nirvana is not my problem in exactly the same way in which Christian Heaven is not my problem. Nirvana, Heaven, the Gods and Goddesses—all good. But because I know I will die, because I live my own death as surely as I live my own life, I inhabit the world of Samsara. "Born like a dream in a dream world," Musō says in a poem, "I shall pass like the morning dew." Asked whether Amida Buddha's Western Paradise really exists, Ikkyū responds with *Amida-hadaka-monogatari,* or *Naked Speaking About Amida,* saying it is *minna mi*—"all within the body." Ezra Pound quotes Confucius, "A man's Paradise is his own good nature."

Here is a poem—an incantation or a sutra perhaps. I made several pilgrimages to Hasedera, the temple of Kannon, bodhisattva of compassion, in Kamakura. There, I had been deeply moved by thousands of little figures of Jizō, Buddha of children and travelers. They had been placed along the steep hillside steps, one by one, by women who had lost children. Some were for infants who died at birth, some for children who had died, but most were for the souls of aborted pregnancies. Often, the little stone figures wore hats or bright bibs, or carried toys. Some had bright umbrellas resting on their shoulders.

Climbing higher, rinse mouth and hands, light incense, and enter the temple of Kannon. In the temple hush, souls of the children become a silent choir, and the four o'clock bell resonates over hills surrounding the city.

Later, outside on the high verandah overlooking the bay, hawks ride long curls of air up and away, over the hills, a few seagulls call, and a faint strand of cloud or mist settles on the horizon. Erotic love, Rexroth used to say, is one of the highest forms of contemplation. Birth-and-love-and-death, Nirvana, Jesus, and the Buddha, even the Temple of Kannon itself—all within the body.

Ten Thousand Sutras
after Hakuin's Meditation Sutra

This body is the body of the Buddha.
Like ice and water, the one is always in the other.

In the middle of the lake
we long for a drink of water.

Adrift in Samsara
we dream of blissful Nirvana.

This body is the body of the Buddha,
this moment an eternity.

Saying I love you, the deed is done—
the name and the deed are one.

With you and without you
the line runs straight—

your body is the body of the Buddha,
there is light beyond the gate.

This love I give to you
is the love that comes from Kannon.

Every breath a sutra.
Going or returning, it's the same.

Our bodies are the bodies of the Buddha,
our names are Kannon's name.

No word can adequately say it,
yet every word must praise it—

in silent meditation
destroying evil karma,

in silent meditation
inhabiting the Dharma—

this body is the body of the Buddha,
your body is the body of the Buddha.

Open arms and eyes to Samsara,
embraced by the thousand arms of Kannon!

In the perfect mind of *vivikta-dharma,*
the truth of solitude,

our body is a temple
not a refuge.

Praise our body
even in Samsara,

our bodies are the body of the Buddha,
our bodies are the body of the Buddha.

"Our body is a temple / not a refuge." The line has been
with me for many years, but I cannot remember whether I

first wrote it or read it. It is Hakuin, of course. The word and the deed become one. Just as there is "Buddha-hood" or enlightenment in lovemaking, there is also *mu,* "nothingness." And there is solitude. And eternal joy in the giving. And monumental grief.

Jizō is really more for us, for those who remain in this cycle of birth and death, than for the children. It is we, ourselves, individually within our own deepest moments of solitude, who seek assurance or solace from without. Jizō? We are Jizō.

In *The Blue Cliff Record,* there is a story of Yun-men who observed that below Dragon Gate, the entrance to Nirvana, there were many gills and scales. He means that many a good monk becomes attached to the idea of non-attachment, clinging to an illusion just as foolish as clinging to a Cadillac. I discussed this koan with Keida Yusuke during one of his visits to my home in Tokyo. Keida-sensei later translated my name into Japanese, selecting characters as follows: *Ha*—wave; *miru*—watch or look; *Sa*—sand or beach; *mu*—dream. Playing with this new name while thinking over our talk about Yun-men, a poem began to take shape.

Watching the Waves
to Keida Yusuke

For fifty years I've drifted,
carried on wandering waves
like a single grain of sand
from a beach a world away.

Yun-men raised his dragon staff:
it swallowed earth and heaven.
Gills and scales at Dragon Gate,
all these years chasing waves!

You return to your cottage
nestled in northern mountains.
I remain in the city,
red dust burning in my eyes.

Moonlight troubles the waters;
mountains and rivers remain.
Blinding light every morning;
in the evening, clouds and rain.

The reader should see, in addition to koan #60 in *The Blue Cliff Record,* Ikkyū Sōjun's poem, "Peach Blossom Waves" in *The Crazy Cloud Anthology.* In the third stanza, the "red dust" refers to evidence of the "pleasures of the world." The first couplet of the fourth stanza refers to Zen "barriers" which remain between myself and "highest perfect enlightenment." The "blinding light" is zazen or silent self-illumination. "Clouds and rain" is an ancient euphemism for lovemaking.

Ryōkan extolled the virtues of incantation of the *nembutsu,* the Buddha's name. Yung Chia says in his *Song of Enlightenment,* "Our illusory unreal body is the Cosmic body." Hakuin says our body is the body of the Buddha.

Making love, sitting zazen, bringing an attitude of devotion to all one's works—seeing one's own carelessness for what it really is when that time comes, I could say, "Sitting zazen improves the quality of one's life." I could say, "If more people sat zazen, the world would be the better for it." But that doesn't mean anything. Jung called for universal individuation. Zen has no missionary tradition.

If Zen practice is to remain abundant, if we continue to embrace its ethics, then we must also participate in feminist zen, we must discover just who are the Matriarchs, and we must learn from them as we have learned from the Patriarchs. Kannon, bodhisattva of compassion, comes from the Chinese Kuan Shih Yin, who in turn comes from the Indian Avalokitesvara. Sometimes masculine, often feminine, Kannon's compassion lies at the heart of my practice. She-who-sees-the-world's-cries. Her listening lies at the heart of her vision.

I seek a balance between masculine and feminine, between social activism and solitude, between Heaven and Earth, between the impossible perfection of grace and the equally impossible sadness of sin.

I seek not the asceticism of zen, but its social engagement; not the activism of the feminist, but her passionate contemplation. What's in the heart of it? Gratitude.

Mr. Kawamura's
Dream Museum

Presently in his mid-fifties, Kawamura Yoichi is an immensely likeable poet far more interested in the well-being of poetry than in his own literary career. Uncomfortable with the thought of life in academia, he chose a career as a refrigeration engineer, all the while writing his own kind of verse. Despite his early association with Kitasono Katue and the avant garde, Kawamura would appear to be very much within the mainstream—and I mean to praise him in so saying.

During our month together in Iwate-ken, the beautiful mountain valley country of northeastern Honshu, we visited museums honoring poets Miyazawa Kenji and Takamura Kotarō, and had tea at Bashō's little teahouse at Chuson-ji, a mountain temple with vistas like no other. He knows the poetry and the poets and the details of their lives. And in the evenings, he often recited to me from the *Man'yoshu,* his wide, intelligent eyes glistening as though he were about to weep over an ancient elegy. To say that he knows the poems doesn't convey a lifetime's engagement with the classics. His voice filled the poems, often only a whisper, like an old man's foot in a dog-eared slipper. It was not only familiar terrain, but a country he thoroughly enjoyed touring.

We first met at a gallery in the Ginza district of Tokyo. We had come to see visual art by poets—drawings, paintings, and calligraphy. Later, over dinner, he apologized for his English, despite his fluency.

"May I call you Sam?"

Of course.

He offered his *meishi,* or personal card, and I offered my own in return. The exchange of cards was formal, each card presented with both hands, inviting the other to read as he receives, each of us bowing slightly as the table permitted.

"My family name is Kawamura," he explained, despite our earlier introduction, "my personal name is Yo-ichi." He emphasized the second syllable of his name. "It means . . ."

"River-village, Ocean-one," I interrupted, looking at the kanji.

He smiled. "You can read kanji?"

A little.

"You will please call me Yoichi?"

I nodded.

"Of course there will be times when we will have to say 'Mr. Hamill' and 'Kawamura-san.' But I despise a lot of needless formality."

I wondered, "There will be times? *What* times does this man plan?" But he was speaking again.

"I want to show you my dream." He looked directly into my eyes, a remarkably American thing to do, and decidedly un-Japanese, considering the circumstances. "I want to show you my dream museum. We are building a museum," he said.

A museum?

"A museum for poetry," he said.

Here in Tokyo?

"Oh no. In Kitakami, in Iwate-ken."

And what do you collect at a poetry museum?

"You have nothing like this in your country?"

Well, we have large collections of books of poetry, and poetry manuscripts, and so forth, but I don't believe we have a poetry *museum,* at least not *as* such. What do you collect at the museum?

"We want books and manuscripts. We also have paintings and sculpture, letters and films and recordings, and photographs."

Then it *is* like a national archive.

"Except that it will be open to everyone, and we will have performances there, ... concerts, and films. And lectures."

Ever the skeptic, I envisioned a little room in the musty corner of some obscure college library. I asked about the size of the poetry museum.

"It isn't built yet."

A-hah! Just as I suspected: a pipe dream. I challenged him to provide details.

"Oh, I can't explain it. You'll have to come visit. I'll *show* it all to you. And you can stay at my cottage in the mountains. I have an *onsen.*"

Sure. Sure. As enticing as the mineral bath sounded, I worried over being drawn into someone else's ambitious schemes.

"You will come? I can take you to see Bashō places. We see *Oku no hosomichi* country. And do you know Takamura Kotarō? Yes? Yes, the Chieko poems! I will take you to see where he lived. And Miyazawa Kenji. You will come?"

Sure. Sure.

Japanese hospitality can sometimes be almost over-whelming to a Westerner, especially to one who has never enjoyed popularity at home. It took another month of coaxing, several dinners, and an exchange of reassurances through the mail, but we finally took the shinkansen to Kitakami.

Riding north from Tokyo on the shinkansen at breath-taking speed, I thought of Bashō on the road, visiting the homes of wealthy poetasters, some good poets and others probably dreadful. Keida-sensei helped me look at a few of Mr. Kawamura's poems, and they seemed complex, and in-teresting. I had liked their rhythms, but then, I liked the rhythms of everything Keida read.

Traveling, one is always vulnerable. I remembered some-thing Octavio Paz had written about Bashō: "To travel is *not* 'to die a little,' but to practice the art of saying goodbye so that, our burden that much lighter, we may learn to receive. Detachments are apprenticeships."

Kawamura-san met us at the station, bursting with enthusiasm. "You have come!" he cried, "Welcome to Kitakami! Welcome to my home." He pointed out the station window. "*Our* mountains!" he proclaimed. "I want this to be your home, too." And then, as we marched through the corridor and down the steps, he turned to Tree. "You can drive?"

"Yes."

"You have international driver's license?"

"Yes."

"Good. You can be our driver!"

We climbed into his tiny red car and drove off into afternoon traffic, heading for the *Nihon Gendai Shiika Bungaku Shiryokan,* the national poetry museum. Kawamura-san grew very quiet. I tried a few questions, only to be told, "You'll see."

We entered a dusty lane and drove along a sagging fence. The lane ended beside a large building which appeared to be a high school, but there were no students, and grass was growing deep in the field beyond the baseball diamond.

"The museum." Kawamura-san said it with finality. He paused a moment. "The museum will be over there," pointing to several acres of weeds. "When they build the museum, they will tear all of this down." His hand swept away the old building. "Let's go in." He paused again. "There will be a pond. And a walkway. Come. I'll show you."

As we exchanged shoes for slippers in the foyer, we were met by Sukegawa Yoshishiko, one of the project directors, who escorted us to his office and introduced us to several women who were busy cataloguing and labeling books. Sukegawa-san having little English, we exchanged greetings in Japanese and asked Kawamura-san to translate henceforth.

I ask how many people work at the museum.

"Just now, ten." Sukegawa-san turns and exchanges

grins with his co-workers. His face is very expressive, the lines at his eyes smiling as broadly as his mouth. He pours tea.

And how many books are on hand?

Mr. Sukegawa says something to a woman at a desk, and she opens a large folder and writes on a slip of paper, which she delivers to Kawamura-san.

"Fifty-six thousand and fifty-six books," he announces, "as of 2 P.M." He smiles. "And there are three thousand, eight hundred and twenty tapes, videos, manuscripts, and other things." He speaks very slowly, almost as if to weigh the numbers as he says them. I write the figures in my notebook. Mr. Sukegawa looks on, smiling beatifically.

"But we've only just begun," Kawamura reminds, "and there'll be much, much more." In Japanese, he asks a staff member to please show us the architect's drawings. We move our cups aside and she spreads a large sheet of paper across the small table.

Bending over the drawings, Kawamura begins to explain, "Here, on the ground floor, we enter, coming around a large pond. The stairwell here is large and will have access for the handicapped. Here, behind the stairwell is the main library with moveable stacks. You will ask the librarian for the books you want to see and they will be delivered. Here, along the sides, are several study rooms."

Kawamura waits patiently while we study the diagram again. "Here," he says, "on the second floor, we will have our theater and gallery area. We plan to have readings and performances here. There are cubicles and lecture halls as well, and the theater will be capable of showing films, videos, slides, . . . all sorts of things."

While Sukegawa-san puts away the architect's drawings and clears away tea cups, I follow Kawamura down the hall and into the stacks. I drift among walls of books, plucking one now and then from the shelf, looking for familiar names or interesting book design. I find Kawamura's poems, a book by Miyoshi Toyoichiro, one of the exhibitors at the visual art by poets opening; and I find books by Takamura Kotarō and Miyazawa Kenji, and a lovely edition of *Midaregami,* tanka by Yosano Akiko written at the turn of the century. There are boxes containing poets' writing brushes and ink sticks, manuscripts, paintings, photographs, boxes of letters, and large cartons of contributions waiting to be catalogued.

Where does it all come from?

"Contributions," Kawamura says simply.

But from where?

"From poets. From friends of poets. From the families of poets. From those who collect poetry and want to see it preserved."

But surely you can't hope to simply collect everything there is.

"Immediately, we want to get all the poetry written since World War Two."

All the *Japanese* poetry.

"Well, of course. But we also want to collect American poetry and European poetry and Russian poetry. Poetry from all over the world."

But the emphasis will be on postwar poetry?

"Yes. For now. But we want to get contributions from other countries."

So desu. That's where I come in.

"Yes," he says softly, sheepishly. "This is now my dream. But now it is someone else's dream. Soon it won't be mine any more." I follow him outside. "See?" he asks, "the museum will be there, in that corner. Maybe you can help the museum get books from America? We want American poets to be here too."

Yes, I would be honored to help in whatever way I can.

Back in Kawamura's tiny red car with Tree at the wheel, we take a country road north and slightly east from the city of Kitakami, heading for Mr. Kawamura's cottage in the mountains of Hanamaki-minami. He points out the To-yosawa River as we cross it. Several fisherman stand in the middle.

"Do you like to catch fish?"

I tell him yes.

"Here," he says, "the river is large. But at *our* cottage, the Toyosawa is very small and the fish are small, but very good to eat. In the morning, we can catch fish."

Thirty minutes later, we arrive at a small cluster of houses.

"Yuguchi-Araisawa, Hanamaki-shi," Kawamura an-nounces, "turn left here." And we drive down a lane barely the width of the car until we come to the last two houses, where we stop. Kawamura leaps from the car, opens the back, and tries to take all the luggage himself. But we man-age to help and carry things into the house.

There are two eight-tatami rooms, a kitchen the size of a walk-in closet, a toilet, and the *onsen,* or mineral hot springs bath. Kawamura has emptied a dresser in one closet so we can unpack. He vanishes into the kitchen, and in fifteen minutes, while we are still unpacking, says, "Let's eat!"

He has set the low table in "his" room and serves sashimi, tempura vegetables, pickled vegetables, and sake. But there is no *gohan,* no cooked rice.

"I don't like rice," he says. "A little now and then, but not three times a day!" He studies our faces for surprise. Seeing approval, he offers, "*Gomenasai,*" a barely audible apology.

Later, the table cleared and a futon spread out in "our" room, we exchange capsule biographies and talk about the various problems we each have had as a result of World War Two—we both have problems with our teeth because of di-etary problems during our childhoods; we each have been touched by racial and religious fanaticism. Mr. Kawamura is the son of a Christian minister in a Buddhist-Shinto culture; I am a Buddhist from a Judeo-Christian nation. We each have made an almost religious commitment to poetry, but have also chosen a life outside the universities.

I inquire about traditional forms in Japanese poetry.

"There are haiku clubs all over Japan," he says.

Does he write haiku?

"Oh, no." Followed by a very pregnant silence.

Does he not like haiku?

He pours more sake, lights a cigarette. Finally, he says very softly, "Haiku began and ended with Bashō."

It is a phrase I have heard many times, and one with which I wholly concur. I offer the opinion that what really makes Bashō great is not simply the haiku, but the haibun, the travel-prose, especially *Oku no hosomichi.* "But what about Issa?" I ask, playing devil's advocate.

"How do you say? Exception proves rule, I think."

And Buson?

"A few, a very few, poems." He has opened both sliding glass doors to this room, and the lights inside attract millions of moths and bugs. He gets up, draws the curtains, pours more sake. Hundreds of tiny dead bugs are falling from the light above the table, and now the whole tabletop takes on a kind of glaze. I put a hand over my sake cup. He explains how haiku grew out of the opening three lines of *haikai no renga,* lines in a syllabic count of 5-7-5. That opening stanza was called *hokku.* The origins of haiku lie in a poetic parlor game. We discuss the *kake-kotoba,* or "pivot word," which makes haiku virtually impossible to translate. We talk about the development of poetic theory before Bashō's time.

"Before Bashō, haiku had almost no seriousness attached to it. But Bashō," he says, letting the name weigh in, "now *there* was a poet!" He looks up, excited, "Would you like to

go to Chuson-ji, would you like to see Hiraizumi? We can
go. I make plans.''

Embarrassed by his generosity, I return to the subject of
poetry. I want to know how the mature poets, those presently in their forties, fifties, and sixties, feel about *tanka,* the
thirty-one-syllable, five-line verse form which dominates
the *Kokinshu* and *Shin-kokinshu.* It was then called *waka,*
which means simply "Japanese poem." It was used to distinguish Japanese poems from those written in Chinese,
called *kanshi.* The waka later became called tanka, indicating a form born in the ancient *uta,* composed in lines of 5-
7-5-7-7 syllables.

"As you probably know," he says, "during the thirties,
tanka as a poetic expression became attached to the worst
elements of Shintoism, to the nationalist cause. Many,
many poets turned away from tanka then, including Takamura Kotarō even though he eventually became a very out-
spoken nationalist. Even your friend, Miyoshi-san, was in-
volved with a group that was a sworn enemy of the tanka.''

Knowing that Miyoshi-san had translated the poetry of
Han Shan into Japanese, I ask whether Miyoshi-san wasn't
in some ways too traditional for the tanka, too much influenced by the Chinese *ch'an* tradition?

Kawamura laughs. "Miyoshi-san is like most Japanese
poets," he says. "When we are young, we want to be rev-
olutionary; we are very experimental. Except for the ancient *choka,* traditional Japanese poetry, as you know, is very
brief. When we are young, we want to try our wings. But
as we grow older, we must relearn the value of the
Man'yoshu and the *Kokinshu.* As we grow older, we understand ancient poets in a new way, and we think that we want
to feel ourselves to be a part of *that* community. So it is with
your friend, Miyoshi-san." Kawamura pours more sake,
lights another cigarette, thinks a moment, then says, "It is

very important for Japanese poets to study kanji. Very important."

I remember Miyoshi-san pausing after giving a reading at the Meguro Museum in Tokyo. After the applause for his beautiful reading, he folded his hands, and very quietly and very firmly implored the audience to pay attention to the study of kanji. Chinese characters are the foundation of Japanese written language. It is easy to rely too heavily upon only the phonetic alphabet, *hiragana,* at the direct expense of a deeper, richer, albeit very difficult tradition.

As we talked on into the late night, I was grateful for the cursory Japanese lessons we'd taken at home and in Tokyo, grateful for the many weeks I'd spent in my study in our house in Ogikubo. Just before turning in, I asked for a poem. He recited a waka by Kakinomoto no Hitomaro, a poem I later translated:

> Dusk, the Omi Sea,
> a lone plover skimming waves,
> and with each soft cry
> my heart too, like dwarf bamboo,
> stirred, longing for bygone days.

Stretched out naked on my futon on a warm summer night, excited like a kid at summer camp, I listen to Tree's deep slow breath in her sleep, to Kawamura's light snore. After months of study in Tokyo, I felt that Hanamaki, like Sanjo and Kamishio, was indeed home. It was good to be in the Tohoku country, the country also called Michinoku.

"To know what precedes and what follows," Confucius says in *The Great Learning,* "is nearly as good as having a head and feet." I thought of Keida-san, alone in Kamishio reading Kamo no Chomei as he had recently written; of Miyoshi-san spending year after year pouring over Han Shan's classical literary Mandarin; of Kawamura-san turning again and again to the *Man'yoshu* for knowledge, for music, for inspiration; and I thought of Bashō's restlessness in Edo, the Tokyo of three hundred years ago, crowded even then.

Those who fail to understand Japanese antiquity are damned to remain in a "contemporary" Japan which is, and will forever be, baffling, severe, indeed as is so often said, inscrutable. The soul of Bashō at the moment of his most penetrating insight is not a different soul from that of van Gogh at the moment of his madness; the visions are both similar and different, but the spirit is one.

A community of artists. The real message of the Modernists, literary and otherwise, is that all art is contemporaneous. That is the Modernist Revolution in sum. But it sounds like Tu Fu speaking with the ghost of Chu Yuan, like Bashō speaking with the ghost of Saigyō, of Takamura Kotarō speaking to Bashō's ghost.

Tree has driven back to the poetry museum, and Kawamura-san and Sukegawa-san are making plans for us to drive south to Hiraizumi to "visit Bashō places." Because Kawamura's car is so small, we will take Mr. Sukegawa's larger one. Mrs. Sukegawa has agreed to join us the next morning.

While they lay plans, I wander again in the stacks, perusing this book and that, very careful to put everything back exactly as I found it. One of the workers comes in, and I ask whether many of the books are by women poets because I've met so few.

"Hai," she says, and tells me more than half the total were written by women. "But we don't keep a count."

She asks whether I know the poetry of Shiraishi Kazuko, and I tell her that I know both the poetry—or as much as has been translated—and the poet. Soon, we are talking about Lady Murasaki, and Izumi Shikibu, and Sei Shonagon, the classic women writers. "In those days," she says, "when poetry was written in *kana,* especially waka, it was said to be written in *onna moji* or 'women's language,' and when it was written in *kanji,* or Chinese, it was called *otoko moji* or 'men's language.' *The Tale of Genji,"* she says, "was written almost entirely in kana."

And in the poetry now, is there often a difference in the language used by men and by women?

"Sometimes. Sometimes men use more kanji. Many kinds of poetry. It is so in your country too?"

It is so in my country, too. But the language is *different, chigaimasu.* We have never had a "women's language."

Discrimination against women has been almost universal, we agree, but different from place to place.

But there is no way to explain the variety of poetry except to repeat, *chigaimasu,* it is different from poet to poet. I tell her that tomorrow we will go to Hiraizumi and have tea where Bashō had tea. We will look at a stone upon which his famous "summer grasses" haiku has been carved. But unless we have read Bashō's *Oku no hosomichi,* and unless we know the history of the nation and of the place, it won't mean much. Because I have studied Bashō, the visit will mean a great deal to me. I try to explain what I mean by "a community of poets."

She covers her mouth with her hand and laughs. "*So desu.* I wish you good journey. You go to visit Bashō's ghost. Please say 'Hello' for me."

Climbing the small mountain to Chuson-ji, I paused along the way to take notes on a tiny rhododendron (*Planchon*) with tiny, rubbery leaves, and a plant identified only as *tessen,* with large lavender blossoms on a vine, plants which would have grown happily at my own home.

Tea at "Bashō's Teahouse," with plenty of his calligraphy on display, his hand strong without being bold like Ikkyū's, his poems snaking down the page. We all sat on the deck in sunshine, took a few pictures, relaxed after the steep climb, and enjoyed the breathtaking view of the valley below. I tried to get a "fix" in my mind about how the Yamato or "Japanese" pushed into this country, driving the Ainu or Emishi further north. It was a country well-suited to give-and-take battles, its mountains and valleys providing hiding places and perfect sites for ambush on a vast scale.

"The glory of three generations of Fujiwaras," Bashō wrote, "is now only an empty dream."

In the twelfth century, Hiraizumi was the cultural center of the Tohoku country, and it was intended to be a "northern Kyoto," a political center laid out in the fashion of the classical Chinese grid. It was ruled by the Fujiwara clan, headed by Fujiwara Kiyohira, under whose direction Chuson-ji was constructed. Established in the ninth century by a Tendai monk, Jikaku Daishi, it had been a small mountain temple like many others. Then Lord Fujiwara had several new temples and pagodas built over a period of two decades, and Chuson-ji was transformed. Additional temples were constructed by his son and grandson respectively during the hundred-year reign of the Fujiwaras.

In the fourteenth century, everything burned down but the Konjiki-dō, or "Golden Hall." The Fujiwaras, like most of the ruling class in Japan at that time, were fascinated with T'ang culture. Consequently, the Fujiwaras took advantage of the Silk Road trade to import Korean, Chinese, Persian, and even Greek arts and materials for construction of their

Golden Hall. Gold, being associated with Amida Jodō, the
Buddha's Paradise, is therefore used not only for covering
the figures (which are almost life-sized), but pillars, floor,
ceiling—everywhere there is gold-leafing. There is also sil-
ver and tusk-ivory, all very heavily ornamented. The Konjiki-dō is viewed through a bulletproof plate of glass with
an armed guard standing nearby.

We climbed on up to the temple complex. The Konjiki-
dō was crowded with high school kids who were as noisy
and rude as all high school kids. Too much gold. Too much
Buddhism and no *sabi*.

In the museum, Tree and Mrs. Sukegawa offered a prayer
to the three Buddhas while I paid homage, off in a corner,
to Kannon. As I knelt before the wooden image, I heard the
high school kids whisper behind me, *"Gaijin!* Look!" Several had tried out a *"Harro!"* on us outside, and we exchanged greetings in Japanese and English, much to their
amusement. As I rose to leave, a girl asked whether I was
Tendai. Not knowing the proper response exactly, I claimed
only "Zenshu," I am a zennist. Soon, there was much more
whispering, and when we left, a fair-sized crowd began to
follow us around, curious about the *Amerika-jin* who had
bowed to Kannon.

We escaped back down the mountain by a back route and
came upon Senju-Kannon-Dō, the tiny ancient temple from
which the Kannon had been removed. Perhaps only twelve
by twelve feet, the wood was soft gray. Further down the
hill, a large pond beside the nunnery. We sat on the stoop
and enjoyed the quiet. Mrs. Sukegawa and Kawamura-san
agreed that Senju-Kannon-Dō was a thousand years old. To
my own tastes, it was a far, far more moving, more *holy,*
place than the Konjiki-dō, or even Chuson-ji itself. I put a
few coins in the offering box, and we walked on down the
hill.

Bashō had remarked on the "burning beauty" of the

Golden Hall. But I couldn't see it that way. I've seen enough Buddhism with armed guards. Whatever's at the heart of my Buddhist or Zennist studies and practice, it has nothing to do with a golden paradise; whatever my *materia mater,* my soul is made of ancient, well-trod wood.

Driving on, we stop at Genbikei Gorge, Motsu-ji, and then on to Takkoku no Iwaya where the Emishi chief, Akurō-o, made his last stand. Akurō-o, Kawamura-san tells us, means "Bad Road King" and was not his name except to the Yamato. To the victors, among other spoils, goes the right to name things. Here, in the entrance to a cavern, the victorious general Sakanoue no Tamuramaro built a great temple after the last battle. Beside the temple, on the stone face of the mountain, his workmen carved a huge relief of the Buddha, Dainichi Nyorai, chipping away the stone by shooting thousands and thousands of arrows.

Some claim Akurō-o was not Ainu, that the people called Emishi or Ezo were not Ainu at all, but were early Yamato or Japanese people who had migrated north in prehistory. The Japanese, like the Chinese, had a tendency, which continues into the present, to categorize anyone from outside the cultural and political center as "foreign." *Ainu* means "hairy people." It has nothing to do with the hairiness of Ainu people, nor with Ezo or Emishi people. The term was imported from China sometime around the seventh or eighth century.

To Kawamura-san, whose ancestry includes Ainu or Emishi (if they are indeed different people), it is a complex and emotional matter. But at rock bottom, to him they are the people of the north country, and are "one people." On the highway back to Kitakami, he recounts the great battles and discusses early life in Tohoku. He has shown us a reconstructed village with thatched-roof houses, early looms and tools, and we begin to understand the complexities of village life in early times.

Back at Kawamura's cottage in Hanamaki, we are joined by Mr. Sukegawa and his son, Masahiro, for a feast. We talk history and Buddhism and practice speaking English with Masahiro until it is late. After the Sukegawas leave for

Kitakami, Tree asleep, I feel Kawamura-san is still disturbed by our trip to Takkoku no Iwaya, and as we wash dishes, I ask.

"My ancestors," he says, then pauses, "my ancestors maybe Ainu, maybe Emishi, maybe Ezo. Is all the same. I think maybe you understand that the Yamato people come from the south, from Nara and Kyoto. My people come from the north." He stacks cups and bowls, then stops a moment. "You understand *chigaimasu?* We are different. . . . We are different people. No matter if we are Japanese." He folds the dish towels and picks up the sake bottle. "One more drink, and I tell you my dream."

We sit side by side in the open doorway. A few night-sounds—a cricket, a few frogs. Silence.

Finally, his thoughts collected, he speaks in a whisper. "Beautiful night. Nights like this, I like to think of ancient people. From them, we learn to eat, to dress, to make home, to sing. Listen!" He cocks his head. "Bashō's frog!" and we burst into laughter.

Then, after another pause and another cup of sake, he continues, speaking softly, very slowly, as if trying to be certain I will understand, "This museum was my dream. It was my dream for many years. It was my dream. But it is not my dream any more. Now it is something else. It belongs to everyone."

He looks up at the sky, but even in the faint light of the doorway, I see tears shimmering in the corners of his eyes. "I am so happy." He swallows hard and lowers his head and eyes. "I am so grateful we can have museum. I buy this house so I can come here and work. But now I know I must have *new* dream."

I think I understand, but fail to see why Takkoku no Iwaya figures into his chosen time and place to speak.

"You do not understand. *Akurō-o. Akurō-o.*" He waits

for the name to sink in. "Bad Road King." Another wait, another cup of sake. "Is not right." He turns to face me. "What do we want in our poems?"

I go a little blank. Music? Sincerity? Intelligence? Insight?

He chuckles. "You study Confucius, *ne?* You read the *Ta Hsueh,* whatchoocallit?"

The Great Learning.

"Yes, *so desu.* You read *The Great Learning.* And in your poems? You want sincerity, *ne?* You want to be sincere."

Yes, I agree.

He thinks a moment. "So."

"So?" I ask.

"So." He looks off into the darkness. "So the poetry museum." He smiles. "Sincerity."

With the curtains open, moonlight pours across my futon. I lie on my back a while, half awake, half dreaming of Tu Fu and Li T'ai-po, Bashō, of a hundred thousand poets who did exactly this. I think of Kawamura Yoichi—"You will call me Yoichi?"—whom I tease by calling in the most honorific terms, "Kawamura-*sama!*"

Playing for the most on a bad pun, Tree and I have named a mountain in Hanamaki-minami *Kawamura-san,* the *san* meaning "mister" or "missus" or "Ms" while also meaning "mountain."

"Ah," we exclaim, "there's rain on Kawamura-san!"

A good man. He told me he felt the only work which really mattered is the work which is given, and given without conditions attached. "That is my dream," he had said. "I dream of a poetry museum. It is a good dream. But the dream doesn't build the museum. All I can do with the dream is give it to someone else. Now I want to give this dream to you. When enough people have this dream, then it will not be my dream anymore. *Then* we can have the museum."

He smiled a wise, sad smile.

"But then I have no dream. What will I do?"

The Ghost of Kotarō

L ying on my back on the tatami mat, bare feet poking through the open glass door and warmed by morning sunshine, I watch a hawk bank and turn, slowly circling the hills above Hanamaki-minami. I have just come from an early morning *onsen,* or natural mineral bath, muscles and mind so relaxed that I'm not certain whether I'm awake or dreaming. Perhaps both. I close my eyes and listen: not a sound but the faint laughter of the Toyosawa River rambling through a rocky section three hundred yards below the house. Opening my eyes again, the world is bathed in yellow light, the hawk a pinpoint, still circling.

Watching the hawk slowly vanish, I remember a poem by Takamura Kotarō, who lived not far from here.

> Chieko Riding the Wind
>
> Chieko, now mad, will not speak
> and only with blue magpies and plovers exchanges signs.
> Along the hill-range of windbreaks
> pine pollen flows everywhere yellow and
> in the clear wind of May, Kujukuri Beach grows hazy.
> Chieko's robe appears and disappears among the pines,
> on the white sands there are truffles growing.
> Gathering them, I
> slowly follow after Chieko.
> The blue magpies and plovers now are her friends.

To Chieko who has already given up being human
this terrifyingly beautiful morning sky is the finest place
   to walk.
Chieko flies.
translation by Hiroaki Sato

It is from a suite of poems about the poet's wife, Chieko, who suffered from severe schizophrenia and died in the late thirties. The poem was written in April 1935, a few years before her death on October 5, 1938. Takamura was a sculptor, the son of a wood-carver. He was a passionate man, deeply interested in Western art, and one of the founders of the *shi* form of poetry, a Modernist poetry of irregular lines. He thought of himself primarily as a sculptor, and he was deeply influenced by Rodin. As a young man, he traveled in Europe. Later, he translated Baudelaire, Rimbaud, Zola, and others.

After the death of his wife, Takamura caught the nationalist fever and wrote terrible, passionate odes about how Japan had "the gods" on its side, poems which would shame him after the war when he was accused of "war responsibilities." During the fire-bombing of Tokyo in April 1945, Takamura's home and most of his art were destroyed. He moved to a northern prefecture, Iwate-ken, but in August of the same year, that home also was bombed. In October, he moved into a hut near the village of Hanamaki, where he remained, working and writing in silence for seven years. It was this hut which was preserved, made into a shrine, and which I visited with Kawamura-san.

The first time we visited Takamura's little house, the sky was overcast. We walked the hundred or so yards from the parking lot to the house along a path beside a pond full of lilies and lotuses, and a well-tilled garden of flowers. A new structure had been erected to protect the little hut within. Kawamura pushed a button and a loudspeaker issued a capsule biography of Kotarō. Through a glass pane, I could see his few tools just as he might leave them, the fireplace, a black iron pot, and several shelves of books on the wall. No one else was around. We walked around the hut, looked at photographs, and read their inscriptions. Then, another hundred yards into the woods, the Kotarō museum. His writing brushes and ink stone, his sculpting tools and gardening tools, and a pair of huge American-made boots, the only ones he could find large enough for his feet. His hands also were enormous. And a couple of studies for sculptures—fleshy, lively, muscular bronze figures very much in the Rodin mold, but with a very different kind of power. I had seen photographs in books, but photographs cannot capture the power of sculpture, especially sculpture which develops such density.

We bought packets of postcards with Chieko's paper cutouts on them. She was herself a distinguished artist, and a rarity: an independent woman. Kotarō helped with household chores. She had kept her own studio, entirely separate from his.

I first read Takamura's tragic poems in Hiroaki Sato's brilliant translation, *Chieko and Other Poems,* while teaching for a couple of weeks on the Indian reservation in Browning, Montana. The only thing deeper than the snow was despair. At night, winds howled and roads closed. I had scheduled three hours per day for studying Tu Fu after my classes ended and had bought *Chieko* for "pleasant reading" in the evenings. From the grim winter of Browning, Montana, I moved on to a prison writing class where the "Chieko poems" became a primary topic. Indeed, I felt I had almost known Kotarō personally. But only in his old age, the way I know our cranky Grampa, Ezra Pound.

Sometime after the war, after moving to his hut near Hanamaki, Takamura Kotarō visited the burnt shell of a temple, Shoan-ji, "in the rustic town called Hanamaki," during the autumn rains on the anniversary of Chieko's

death. He felt the power of his own humility, and he felt
Chieko had "burned up" for him. And in the last of the
"Chieko poems" Sato has given, "Soliloquy on a Night of
Blizzard," the poet at age sixty-seven considers his art, his
purpose. "On a night like this the rats stay put," he says.
"What comes out of this harsh inhumanity, / a barely per-
ceptible fragrance, is perhaps / what they call god's rhyme. /
Though senility wouldn't be too good."

"Beauty," Aubrey Beardsley said, "is difficult." Certainly it was difficult for Takamura Kotarō with his own vision of "inhumanity," which in some ways summons the
ghost of Robinson Jeffers, his own steely eyes fixed on the
horizon of the Pacific. "Beauty makes outcasts of us all,"
some ancient Chinese poet wrote.

Yesterday, driving back from another visit to the Kotarō
museum with Kawamura, Keida Yusuke, and Tree, Keida
told us Raymond Carver had died. I had known Carver during a particularly wretched time in Santa Barbara, and again
later, when he was sober, in Montana. Tree wept. Carver
was a beautiful man who, at the end, no longer felt like an
outcast. He had made something beautiful and accessible.
Later, hiking along the Toyosawa River, I thought about
Carver, Takamura, any number of writers and artists I had
known. I remembered the composer, Jon Brower, with
whom I collaborated, and how he didn't want to meet me
because his face was covered with sores brought on by
AIDS. So we never met. A photograph in *Newsweek* por-
trayed a handsome young man with dark, penetrating eyes.

And Takamura—I couldn't get over it—bore a startling
resemblance to John Huston. But of course, that should be
said the other way around: John Huston came to bear strik-
ing resemblance to Takamura Kotarō. Something in the
powerful set of the jaw, combined with a raw vitality which
can be seen in the eyes.

A mile upriver from Kawamura's cottage, we came to Usuginu Falls hidden deep in a cove on a sharp hillside. The waterfall is perhaps thirty feet high, the river thin. When Tree stood under it, she couldn't breathe, but it was not sufficient to buckle her knees. She was beautiful there on the mountainside, standing under the waterfall while we took pictures and laughed. I thought then about Chieko's momentary happiness, how lovely she must have been during times of sanity. We had each perhaps been touched in some very private way by Kotarō's poetry, by Chieko's life and death, and we had each been touched by Ray Carver. There, for a while, we played along the waterfall like children.

Keida-san left before dawn, taking the train back to his own version of the north country, the "snow country" of Niigata. Tree and Kawamura-san sleep peacefully. Limp from my bath, I warm my feet in the first sun, read a poem or two about Chieko, daydream, utterly happy and just a little sad. The world is unspeakably brilliant, freshly bathed. A hawk disappears down the sky.

What he sought was what the object became, whether sculpture or poetry. Only when engaged in the process of its becoming was the artist fully alive. The poem must reveal itself to the poet. If the poet makes no discovery in the course of making the poem, how can there be anything for anyone else to discover unless poetry is merely a riddle? He adored the rough simplicity of prehistoric Japanese *haniwa* clay figures, seeing in them a prototype for all Japanese aesthetics. He objected strenuously to the Japanese tendency to admire the fragility and perishability of beauty. *Aware* had been reduced to mere pathos, *yugen* to mere technique. In a New Year's Day poem from 1950, he wrote (in Makoto Ueda's translation):

> "Stop playing Nippon's music in the minor mode.
> Things gloomy, doleful,
> shady, forlorn, destitute,
> and yet with humble
> and quiet grace,
> making one see Mount Sumeru in a sesame seed—
> those 'beautiful' things:
> discard them all and raise your eyes higher...."

Like his contemporary, Robinson Jeffers, he placed his deepest faith in Nature. Like Nature, Kotarō felt himself to be in a perpetual state of becoming, a state which was clarified and heightened during the process of revealing art. "No artist," he said, "need think about the end product in advance." And what is the antidote to the degradation of severe beauty? "Sincerity."

As a young man, he had been a member of a "decadent" group which advocated every excess. But he soon tired of the scene, and left for Hokkaido to farm. That plan also quickly folded. He searched. They were difficult years, not unlike the early years of Bashō. In Chieko, he found Nature, he found, he believed, his oracle.

Kotarō wrote a small memoir, "The Latter Half of Chieko's Life," in 1950. I quote only one paragraph:

"There is nothing more encouraging to an artist than the consciousness of having one person who will examine his creation with the eyes of fervent love. There is no better latent power than this to assure the completion of something you want to create. The result of the creation might possibly become a public possession. But usually the creator's mind is already full of the all-encompassing desire to have his creation seen by this one person. I had such a person in my wife Chieko. The feeling of emptiness that I had at the time of Chieko's death was therefore equivalent to a world of nothingness. Even though there were things that I wanted to make, I didn't feel like making them, because I knew that in this world there were no longer those loving eyes to see them. After several months of struggle, a certain accident on a night of the full moon made me feel keenly that Chieko had in fact become a universal being to me through her loss of individual being. From then on I felt Chieko's breathing much closer; she became, so to speak, one who stayed with me, and the sensation that she was someone eternal to me became stronger. Thus I regained a measure of calmness, mental health, and, once again, an incentive to work. Now when I finish a day's work, view the result, and look back saying, 'What do you think?' Chieko is there without fail. Chieko is everywhere."

—*from* Chieko's Sky, *translation by Soichi Furuta*

Here, where the old iron bridge crosses the little river, I sit with legs dangling over the edge, watching dozens of small dark fish, *masu,* or brown trout, swim in and out of moss-covered rocky caverns fifteen feet below. The air is alive with the electric buzz of *higurashi.* Cicadas. I slip a hook into the soft flesh of a *budomushi,* a "grape worm," and drop the line over the edge. It sinks slowly to the bottom, disappearing into the shadows. Here, the river is small and calm. Most of the larger fish are several hundred yards up the stream, behind the flood control dam. Working the line, one catches small fish here, perhaps the tastiest for sashimi. But I'm not working the line. I lay the pole beside me and watch the fish below.

Kawamura-san has been out picking fern shoots and mushrooms, and has gone back to the kitchen to prepare *mozuku,* a delicious fine seaweed in vinegar, sugar, and lime juice.

Late morning sunlight, sweaty back, it's a terrible time in every respect to be fishing. Keida Yusuke often goes down to the little river behind his cottage and fishes in the late afternoon before returning to his papers.

I ask what he catches.

"No fish. . . . I fish for water."

In March 1945, Tokyo was bombed. Four thousand *tons* of bombs fell on Tokyo alone. Emperor Hirohito, realizing Japan's defeat, attempted to negotiate a peace. But just as he had proven almost powerless against the military establishment led by Tojo, his efforts were fruitless. Atomic bombs fell on Hiroshima and Nagasaki in August. The Japanese military finally offered unconditional surrender.

The Son of Heaven was no longer immortal. When he broadcast Japan's surrender over the radio, it was the first time the public had heard his voice. But if he had truly been the Son of Heaven, why had he failed to prohibit the war?

Japan was not terribly prosperous. Shinto had become a nationalist religion. The Japanese, isolated for their entire history, were fearful. Like nearly every war, the war in the Pacific hinged on fear, racism, and religious bigotry founded upon the certainty that God (or the Gods) is on "our" side. The fear, the racism, and the religious bigotry of Japan were mirrored almost perfectly by the United States.

The Son of Heaven quickly became mortal. And at the end of the war, he asked to meet with General MacArthur. The general assumed the Emperor would come to beg for his life. But Hirohito offered his own life in return for mercy for his defeated people. The "Reign of Enlightened Peace" thus became an era of war and defeat and rebuilding and subsequent prosperity like the nation, or any nation, had never witnessed before.

And now the emperor is dying. There are blood transfusions. He is in his mid-eighties and can barely get around. If he takes a little walk, he makes major news. But he persists in his interest in gardening and especially in marine biology.

I spend the afternoon at the *Go* board with Yoichi, talking about the war, about the emperor, and about Kotarō. We each remember the lessons of profound racism we were taught as children. I ask what he thinks will happen when the emperor dies.

"An end," he says. "A beginning." We play a few moves on the board, and then he continues, "But not much will change."

I get up and dig out a book from my pack, Lucien Stryk's translations of Takahashi Shinkichi, *Triumph of the Sparrow,* to read my friend a poem:

Wind Among the Pines

The wind blows hard among the pines
Toward the beginning
Of an endless past.
Listen: you've heard everything.

In December 1911, Takamura Kotarō was struggling with his poetry. He wanted to write as he spoke, *in the vernacular.* But no Japanese poet had managed such a thing. As winter closed in on Tokyo, he met a twenty-five-year-old painter, Naganuma Chieko, who was unlike anyone Kotarō had ever met. She was a member of a feminist group. She had her own ideas about art and about life.

Kotarō was at work on a poem which eventually filled 102 lines, a poem called "The Journey," which became the title poem to his first book. He had accomplished his task: the poems were indeed written in the vernacular. His syntax was direct and uncluttered. But he was dissatisfied with the title poem. It said too much. He began carving not with the eye and ear of the poet, but with the sure hands of a wood-carver. A sentence, a line, a word, ... chips fell slowly, regularly away from the body of the poem. Writing his poem, he surely thought of Bashō: "Each day is a journey, and the journey itself is home." Kotarō had written a haiku journal, travelogues, and tanka. But he wanted to emulate Bashō, perhaps; he certainly did not intend to imitate him. He continued to carve his poem.

Three years later to the month, Kotarō and Chieko were married. The following fifteen years were to be the happiest of their lives. And then the madness, and then the agony began.

Chieko has been dead fifty years. Kotarō has been dead thirty years. The title poem to his first book, published three-quarters of a century ago, is known only as a brief lyric, nine lines in length, a prayer to "Father Nature" to strengthen the poet for his journey. And of those nine lines, the opening couplet summarizes a life, it summons the entire critical vocabulary of Japanese poetry in a few common words—Kotarō's *sabi,* his *kokoro,* his supreme resignation and powerful humanism in the tradition of Kamo no Chomei and Bashō and Ryōkan.

> No road leads the way.
> The road follows behind.

Bibliography

Aitken, Robert. *The Mind of Clover: Essays in Zen Buddhism.* San Francisco: North Point Press, 1984. Essays by an American Zen master; excellent.

Aitken, Robert. *Taking the Path of Zen: Essays by Robert Aitken.* San Francisco: North Point Press, 1982. Excellent.

Aitken, Robert. *A Zen Wave: Bashō's Haiku and Zen.* New York and Tokyo: Weatherhill, 1978. Essential.

Arntzen, Sonja, trans. *Ikkyū and the Crazy Cloud Anthology.* Foreword by Shuichi Kato. Tokyo: University of Tokyo Press, 1986. The poems lack a poet's touch, but essential reading nonetheless.

Bashō, Matsuo. *The Narrow Road to the Deep North and Other Travel Sketches.* Translated by Nobuyuki Yuasa. New York: Penguin Books, 1986. Good.

Bellah, Robert. *Tokugawa Religion.* Free Press, 1957. A very good study.

Berg, Stephen. *Crow with No Mouth: Ikkyū, 15th Century Zen Master.* Preface by Lucien Stryk. Port Townsend, Washington: Copper Canyon Press, 1989. Excellent.

Blofeld, John, trans. *The Zen Teaching of Hui Hai.* Talks on "sudden illumination" with a helpful introduction by a great scholar-translator; excellent.

Bly, Robert, trans. *Bashō.* San Francisco: Cranium Press, 1972. Beautiful limited edition printed by Clifford Burke.

Blyth, R. H. *Edo Satirical Verse Anthologies.* Tokyo: The Hokuseido Press, 1961. This is one to read just for the fun of it.

Blyth, R. H. *Haiku.* 5 vols. Tokyo: The Hokuseido Press, 1949. Excellent.

Blyth, R. H. *A History of Haiku.* 2 vols. Tokyo: The Hokuseido Press, 1964. Excellent.

Blyth, R. H. *Senryu: Japanese Satirical Verse*. Tokyo: The Hokuseido
    Press, 1949. Excellent.

Blyth, R. H. *Zen and Zen Classics*. 5 vols. Tokyo: The Hokuseido
    Press; Rutland, Vermont, and Tokyo: Charles E. Tuttle Com-
    pany, 1960. Blyth was a great man and a daring zennist; his range
    of understanding is profound.

Bownas, Geoffrey, and Anthony Thwaite, trans. *The Penguin Book of
    Japanese Verse*. Introduction by Geoffrey Bownas. New York:
    Penguin Books, 1964. Good.

Britton, Dorothy, trans. *A Haiku Journey, Bashō's Narrow Road to a
    Far Province*. Tokyo, New York, and San Francisco: Kodansha
    International, 1986. Fair.

Buchanan, Daniel Crump. *Japanese Proverbs and Sayings*. Tokyo:
    Enderle Book Company, 1965. Like most such collections,
    charming, interesting.

Cleary, Thomas, and J. C. Cleary, trans. *The Blue Cliff Record*. 3
    vols. Boston: Shambala Publications, Inc., 1977. Essential.

Conze, Edward, trans. *Buddhist Wisdom Books*. New York: Harper
    & Row, Publishers, 1972. Translations from the Sanskrit of the
    Diamond Sutra and the *Heart Sutra;* essential.

Conze, Edward, trans. *The Perfection of Wisdom in Eight Thousand
    Lines*. Berkeley: Four Seasons, 1975. Essential.

Corman, Cid. *One Man's Moon: 50 Haiku by Bashō, Buson, Issa,
    Hakuin, Shiki, Santoka*. Frankfort, Kentucky: Gnomon Press,
    1984. Excellent.

Corman, Cid, and Kamaike Susumu, trans. *Back Roads to Far Towns:
    Bashō's Oku-No-Hosomichi*. New York: Grossman Publishers,
    Inc., 1968. Reissued by White Pine Press, 1986. Essential.

Covell, Jon Carter, and Abbott Sobin. *Unraveling Zen's Red Thread:
    Ikkyū's Controversial Way*. Elizabeth, New Jersey: Yamada, Hol-
    lym International, 1980.

Crihfield, Liza. *Ko-Uta: "Little Songs" of the Geisha World*. Rutland,
    Vermont, and Tokyo: Charles E. Tuttle Company, 1979.
    Delightful.

Doe, Paula. *A Warbler's Song at Dusk: The Life and Work of Otoma
    Yakamochi (718–785)*. Berkeley, Los Angeles, and London: Uni-
    versity of California Press, 1982. Excellent scholarly study.

Dumoulin, Heinrich. *A History of Zen Buddhism*. Translated from
    the German by Paul Prachey. New York: Random House, 1963.
    Excellent.

Dumoulin, Heinrich. *Zen Buddhism: A History.* 2 vols. Translated from the German by James W. Heisig and Paul Knitter. New York: Macmillan Publishing Company, Inc., 1988. Excellent.

Epp, Robert, trans. *Treelike: The Poetry of Kinoshita Yuji.* Preface by Ooka Makoto. Rochester, Michigan: Katydid Books, Oakland University, 1982.

Fenollosa, Ernest. *Epochs of Chinese & Japanese Art: An Outline History of East Asiatic Design.* 2 vols. New York: Dover Publications, Inc., 1963.

French, Joseph Lewis, ed. *Lotus and Chrysanthemum.* Boni and Liveright, 1927. Good in its time; an interesting curiosity.

Fuller, Ruth, and Isshu Miura Sasaki, trans. *The Zen Koan: Its History and Use in Rinzai Zen.* San Diego, New York, and London: Harcourt Brace Jovanovich, Publishers, 1965. A classic.

Galt, Tom, trans. *The Little Treasury of One Hundred People, One Poem Each, Compiled by Fujiwara no Sadaie.* Princeton: Princeton University Press, 1982.

Gibson, Morgan, and Hiroshi Murakami, trans. *Tantric Poetry of Kukai.* Bangkok: Mahachulalongkorn Buddhist University Press, 1982. Excellent.

Goldstein, Sanford, and Seishi Shinoda, trans. *Tangled Hair: Selected Tanka from Midaregami by Akiko Yosano.* Rutland, Vermont, and Tokyo: Charles E. Tuttle Company, 1987. They've reordered her lines, and the translations lack a poet's touch, but it's the only large Yosano Akiko collection in English; essential.

Guest, Harry, Lynn Guest, and Kajima Shozo, trans. *Post-War Japanese Poetry.* New York: Penguin Books, 1972. A survey; good.

Hagiwara, Sakutaro. *Face at the Bottom of the World and Other Poems.* Translated by Graeme Wilson. Rutland, Vermont, and Tokyo: Charles E. Tuttle Company, 1969.

Hamill, Sam. *A Dragon in the Clouds: Poems and Translations by Sam Hamill.* Seattle: Broken Moon Press, 1989.

Hearn, Lafcadio. *Glimpses of Unfamiliar Japan.* Rutland, Vermont, and Tokyo: Charles E. Tuttle Company, 1974.

Hearn, Lafcadio, trans. *Japanese Lyrics.* Boston: Houghton Mifflin Company, 1915.

Hearn, Lafcadio. *Kokoro: Hints and Echoes of Japanese Inner Life.* Rutland, Vermont, and Tokyo: Charles E. Tuttle Company, 1972. Still very interesting after nearly one hundred years.

Hersey, John. *Hiroshima.* New York: Alfred A. Knopf, Inc., 1946.

Hirshfield, Jane, and Mariko Aratani, trans. *The Ink Dark Moon: Love Poems by Ono No Komachi and Izumi Shikibu, Women of the Ancient Court of Japan*. New York: Charles Scribner's Sons, 1988. Good.

Hoffmann, Yoel, trans. *Japanese Death Poems*. Rutland, Vermont, and Tokyo: Charles E. Tuttle Company, 1986.

Hoffmann, Yoel, trans. *The Sound of the One Hand: 281 Zen Koans with Answers*. New York: Basic Books, 1975. Despite the astonishing subtitle, a good book.

Honda, H. H., trans. *Man'yoshu*. Tokyo: The Hokuseido Press, 1961. Bilingual.

Honda, H. H. *The Poetry of Ishikawa Takuboku*. Tokyo: The Hokuseido Press, 1959. Bilingual.

Kapleau, Philip, ed. and trans. *The Three Pillars of Zen: Teaching, Practice, and Enlightenment*. Boston: Beacon Press, 1967. Excellent.

Kapleau, Philip. *Zen: Dawn in the West*. Foreword by Albert Low. Garden City, New York: Anchor Press/Doubleday, 1979. Excellent.

Kato, Shuichi. *A History of Japanese Literature*. 3 vols. Translated by Don Sanderson. Tokyo, New York, and San Francisco: Kodansha International, 1983. Lacks depth and is grossly over-priced.

Keene, Donald, ed. *Anthology of Japanese Literature: From the Earliest Era to the Mid-Nineteenth Century*. New York: Grove Press, Inc., 1955. Excellent.

Keene, Donald, trans. *Essays in Idleness: The Tsurezuregusa of Kenko*. New York: Columbia University Press, 1967. Essential.

Keene, Donald. *Some Japanese Portraits*. Tokyo, New York, and San Francisco: Kodansha International, 1978. Historical portraits; excellent.

Keene, Donald. *World Within Walls: Japanese Literature of the Pre-Modern Era (1600–1867)*. New York: Grove Press, Inc., 1976. Excellent.

Kim, Hee-jin. *Dogen Kigen: Mystical Realist*. Tucson: University of Arizona Press, 1987. Excellent.

Kirimura, Yasuji. *Fundamentals of Buddhism*. Translated by *Seikyo Times*. Nichiren Shoshu International Center, 1977. Useful introductory book.

Kodama, Sanehide. *American Poetry and Japanese Culture*. Hamden, Connecticut: Archon Books, The Shoe String Press, Inc., 1984. Essential.

Kubose, Gyomay M. *Zen Koans.* Chicago: Regnery Company, 1973. Good.

Kusano, Shimpei. *asking myself answering myself.* Translated by Cid Corman. New York: New Directions Books, 1984.

Kusano, Shimpei. *frogs & others.* Translated by Cid Corman. Tokyo: Mushinsha Grossman, 1969.

LaFleur, William R. *The Karma of Words.* Berkeley, Los Angeles, and London: University of California Press, 1983. Brilliant and indispensable.

LaFleur, William R., trans. *Mirror for the Moon: A Selection of Poems by Saigyō (1118–1190).* Foreword by Gary Snyder. New York: New Directions Books, 1978. Essential.

Leggett, Trevor, trans. *A First Zen Reader.* Rutland, Vermont, and Tokyo: Charles E. Tuttle Company, 1988. Good.

Leggett, Trevor, trans. *A Second Zen Reader.* Rutland, Vermont, and Tokyo: Charles E. Tuttle Company, 1988. Good.

Leggett, Trevor, trans. *The Tiger's Cave and Translations of Other Zen Writings.* Rutland, Vermont, and Tokyo: Charles E. Tuttle Company, 1988. Good.

Leggett, Trevor, trans. *Zen and the Way.* Rutland, Vermont, and Tokyo: Charles E. Tuttle Company, 1988. Good.

Levy, Howard S., trans. *Minemoto no Sanetomo.* Pasadena, California: Langstaff Books. Bilingual.

Levy, Howard S., trans. *Saigyō: 100 Love Poems.* Pasadena, California: Langstaff Books. Bilingual.

Levy, Howard S., trans. *Saigyō: 100 More Love Poems.* Pasadena, California: Langstaff Books. Bilingual.

Levy, Ian Hideo, trans. *Man'yoshu.* vol. 1. Tokyo: University of Tokyo Press; Princeton: Princeton University Press, 1982. Essential.

Mackenzie, Lewis, trans. *The Autumn Wind: Poems of Issa.* Tokyo, New York, and San Francisco: Kodansha International, 1984. Good.

Maloney, Dennis, trans. *Dusk Lingers: Haiku of Issa.* Fredonia, New York: White Pine Press, 1986. Good, but brief.

Maloney, Dennis, and Hide Oshiro, trans. *Tangled Hair: Love Poems of Yosano Akiko.* Fredonia, New York: White Pine Press, 1987. Small, but good.

Masunaga, Reiho. *A Primer of Soto Zen: A Translation of Dogen's "Shonogenzo Zuimonki."* Honolulu: East-West Center Press, 1971. Excellent.

McCandless, Ruth Strout, and Nyogen Senzaki, ed. and trans.
    Buddhism and Zen. Foreword by Robert Aitken. San Fran-
    cisco: North Point Press, 1987. Excellent.

McCullough, Helen Craig, trans. *Kokin Wakashu: The First Imperial
    Anthology of Japanese Poetry.* Stanford: Stanford University Press,
    1985.

McCullough, Helen Craig, trans. *Yoshitsune.* Stanford: Stanford
    University Press, 1971. A history of the turbulent fifteenth
    century, essential to understanding Bashō's *Oku no hosomichi;*
    excellent.

Merton, Thomas. *Zen and the Birds of Appetite.* New York: New
    Directions Books, 1968. Essays; excellent.

Merwin, W. S., and Soiku Shigematsu, trans. *Sun at Midnight: Poems
    and Sermons by Muso Soseki.* Introduction by W. S. Merwin. San
    Francisco: North Point Press, 1989. Essential.

Miner, Earl. *An Introduction to Japanese Court Poetry.* Stanford: Stan-
    ford University Press, 1968. Excellent.

Miner, Earl, ed. and trans. *Japanese Poetic Diaries.* Berkeley, Los
    Angeles, and London: University of California Press, 1969.
    Includes a translation of *Oku no hosomichi;* essential.

Miner, Earl, and Hiroko Odagiri, trans. *The Monkey's Straw Raincoat
    and Other Poetry of the Bashō School.* Princeton: Princeton Univer-
    sity Press, 1981. Excellent scholarly translation.

Miyazawa, Kenji. *A Future of Ice: Poems and Stories of a Japanese
    Buddhist.* Translated by Hiroaki Sato. San Francisco: North
    Point Press, 1989.

Miyazawa, Kenji. *Winds from Afar.* Translated by John Bester.
    Tokyo, New York, and San Francisco: Kodansha International,
    1972. Wonderful stories.

Ono, Sokyo. *Shinto: The Kami Way.* Rutland, Vermont, and Tokyo:
    Charles E. Tuttle Company, 1962. Excellent introduction.

Philippi, Donald L., trans. *Kojiki.* Princeton: Princeton University
    Press; Tokyo: University of Tokyo Press, 1969. The "Record of
    Ancient Things," and the earliest "history" of Japan; excellent.

Philippi, Donald L., trans. *Songs of Gods, Songs of Humans: Ainu
    Epics.* Princeton: Princeton University Press; Tokyo: University
    of Tokyo Press, 1979. Excellent.

Philippi, Donald L., trans. *This Wine of Peace, This Wine of Laughter.*
    Tokyo: Mushinsha Grossman, 1968. The poetry of the pre-
    Man'yoshu epoch; excellent.

The Poetry of Living Japan: An Anthology. Introduction by Takamichi Ninomiya and D. J. Enright. New York: Grove Press, Inc., 1957.

Pollack, David. *Zen Poems of the Five Mountains.* Decatur, Georgia, and New York: The Crossroad Publishing Company and Scholars Press, 1985. Very good.

Pound, Ezra. *Collected Translations.* New York: New Directions Books, 1953. Essential.

Pound, Ezra, and Ernest Fenollosa. *The Classic Noh Theatre of Japan.* New York: New Directions Books, 1959. Essential.

Reps, Paul, ed. *Zen Flesh, Zen Bones.* Rutland, Vermont, and Tokyo: Charles E. Tuttle Company, 1957. Zen stories and dialogues; a little masterpiece.

Rexroth, Kenneth, ed. *The Buddhist Writings of Lafcadio Hearn.* Introduction by Kenneth Rexroth. Santa Barbara, California: Ross-Erikson, Inc., 1977. Excellent.

Rexroth, Kenneth. *The Elastic Retort.* New York: Seabury Press, 1973.

Rexroth, Kenneth. *With Eye and Ear.* New York: Herder and Herder, 1970.

Rexroth, Kenneth, trans. *One Hundred More Poems from the Japanese.* New York: New Directions Books, 1976. Essential.

Rexroth, Kenneth, trans. *One Hundred Poems from the Japanese.* New York: New Directions Books, 1955. Essential.

Rexroth, Kenneth, and Ikuko Atsumi, ed. and trans. *The Burning Heart: Women Poets of Japan.* New York: A Continuum Book, The Seabury Press, 1977. Reissued as *Women Poets of Japan.* New York: New Directions Books, 1982. Essential.

Rexroth, Kenneth, Ikuko Atsumi, John Solt, Carol Tinker, and Yasuyo Morita, trans. *Seasons of Sacred Lust: The Selected Poems of Kazuko Shiraishi.* New York: New Directions Books, 1978. Japan's best-known "Beat" poet; a terrific performer.

Rodd, Laurel Rasplica, and Mary Catherine Henkenius, trans. *Kokinshu.* Tokyo: University of Tokyo Press; Princeton: Princeton University Press, 1984. Very good.

Ross, Nancy Wilson, ed. *The World of Zen: An East-West Anthology.* Introduction by Nancy Wilson Ross. New York: Random House, 1960. Excellent.

Ryuichi, Tamura. *Dead Languages: Selected Poems 1946–1984.* Translated by Christopher Drake. Rochester, Michigan: Katydid Books, Oakland University, 1984. Good.

Sanford, James H. *Zen-Man Ikkyū*. Chico, California: Scholars Press, 1981. Scholarly, and far better than the title suggests.

Sansom, George. *A History of Japan to 1334*. Stanford: Stanford University Press, 1958. History text; excellent.

Sato, Hiroaki, trans. *A Bunch of Keys: Selected Poems by Matsuo Takahashi*. Introduction by Robert Peters. Trumansburg, New York: The Crossing Press, 1984. Excellent.

Sato, Hiroaki, trans. *Chieko and Other Poems of Takamura Kotarō*. Honolulu: The University of Hawaii Press, 1980. Essential.

Sato, Hiroaki, trans. *Spring & Asura: Poems of Kenji Miyazawa*. Chicago: Chicago Review Press, 1973. Excellent.

Sekimori, Gaynor, trans. *Hibakusha: Survivors of Hiroshima and Nagasaki*. Tokyo: Koseu Publishing, 1986.

Senzaki, Nyogen, and Ruth Strout McCandless, trans. *The Iron Flute: 100 Zen Koan*. Rutland, Vermont, and Tokyo: Charles E. Tuttle Company, 1961. A classic.

Shibayama, Abbott Zankei. *A Flower Does Not Talk: Zen Essays by Abbott Zankei Shibayama*. Rutland, Vermont, and Tokyo: Charles E. Tuttle Company, 1970. Excellent.

Shigematsu, Soiku, trans. *A Zen Forest: Sayings of the Masters*. Foreword by Gary Snyder. New York and Tokyo: Weatherhill, 1981. Reissued by North Point Press; essential.

Shigematsu, Soiku, trans. *Zen Harvest: Japanese Zen Folk Sayings*. San Francisco: North Point Press, 1988.

Shiraishi, Kazuko. *Cuttack*. Translated by John Solt and Shoshi-Yamada. 1985.

Shiraishi, Kazuko. *Little Planet, The Goanna God*. Translated by Allen Ginsberg, Roger Pulvers, and Shoshi-Yamada. 1985.

Snyder, Gary. *The Back Country*. New York: New Directions Books, 1968. Includes poems of Kenji Miyazawa; excellent.

Solt, John, trans. *Burning Meditation: Poems by Kazuko Shiraishi*. Tokyo: Seichisha, 1988. A beautiful limited edition.

Stevens, John, trans. *One Robe, One Bowl: The Zen Poetry of Ryōkan*. New York and Tokyo: Weatherhill, 1977. Excellent.

Stryk, Lucien. *Encounter with Zen*. Chicago: The Swallow Press, Inc., 1981. Writings on poetry and Zen; excellent.

Stryk, Lucien, trans. *On Love and Barley: Haiku of Bashō*. New York: Penguin Books, 1985. Excellent.

Stryk, Lucien, ed. and trans. *Zen: Poems, Prayers, Sermons, Anecdotes, Interviews*. New York: Anchor Books, 1965. Excellent.

Stryk, Lucien, and Takashi Ikemoto, trans. *Afterimages: Zen Poems of Shinkichi Takahashi.* Chicago: The Swallow Press, Inc., 1970. Excellent.

Stryk, Lucien, and Takashi Ikemoto, trans. *The Duckweed Way: Haiku of Issa.* Derry, Pennsylvania: The Rook Press, 1977. Excellent, but brief.

Stryk, Lucien, and Takashi Ikemoto, trans. *Triumph of the Sparrow: Zen Poems of Shinkichi Takahashi.* Urbana, Illinois, and Chicago: University of Illinois Press, 1986. A contemporary Zen master and a great poet; essential.

Suzuki, D. T. *Essays.* New York: Samuel Weiser Inc., 1971. Along with the *Manual of Zen Buddhism, Living by Zen,* and *Zen Doctrine of No Mind,* constitutes the essential Suzuki.

Suzuki, D. T. *Sengai: The Zen Master.* Greenwich, Connecticut: New York Graphic Society, 1971. Excellent.

Suzuki, D. T. *The Training of the Zen Buddhist Monk.* New York: University Books, 1965. Excellent.

Swain, David L. *Hiroshima.* Notes by Kenzaburo Oe. Tokyo: YMCA Press, 1981.

Tadayoshi, Onuma, trans. *Celebration in Darkness: Selected Poems of Yoshioka Minoru.* Introduction by Ooka Makoto. Rochester, Michigan: Katydid Books, Oakland University, 1985.

Tadayoshi, Onuma, trans. *Stranger's Sky: Selected Poems of Iijima Koichi.* Introduction by Ooka Makoto. Rochester, Michigan: Katydid Books, Oakland University, 1985.

Takahashi, Matsuo. *Poems of a Penisist.* Translated by Hiroaki Sato. Chicago: Chicago Review Press, 1975. A contemporary gay poet with a wild imagination and an international vision; excellent.

Takamura, Kotarō. *Chieko's Sky.* Translated by Soichi Furuta. Tokyo, New York, and San Francisco: Kodansha International, 1978. Good.

Tanahashi, Kazuaki. *Penetrating Laughter: Hakuin's Zen and Art.* Woodstock, New York: The Overlook Press, 1984. Excellent.

Tanikawa, Shuntarō. *Coca-Cola Lessons.* Translated by William I. Elliott and Kazuo Kawamura. Portland, Oregon: Prescott Street Press, 1986. Very good.

Tanikawa, Shuntarō. *Floating the River in Melancholy.* Translated by William I. Elliott and Kazuo Kawamura. Portland, Oregon: Prescott Street Press, 1989.

Tanikawa, Shuntarō. *At Midnight in the Kitchen I Just Wanted to Talk to You*. Translated by William I. Elliott and Kazuo Kawamura. Foreword by Bonnie R. Crown. Portland, Oregon: Prescott Street Press, 1980. Excellent.

Tanikawa, Shuntarō. *With Silence My Companion*. Translated by William I. Elliott and Kazuo Kawamura. Portland, Oregon: Prescott Street Press, 1975. Excellent.

Tanizaki, Junichiro. *In Praise of Shadows*. Translated by Thomas J. Harper and Edward G. Seidensticker. Leete's Island Books, 1977. A powerful and important essay; excellent.

Tsunoda, Ryusaku, William Theodore de Bary, and Donald Keene, ed. *Sources of Japanese Tradition*. New York: Columbia University Press, 1958. A great textbook.

Uchiyama, Kosho Roshi. *Approach to Zen*. San Francisco and Tokyo: Japan Publications, 1973. Talks on zazen practice; excellent.

Ueda, Makoto. *Matsuo Bashō: Master Haiku Poet*. Tokyo, New York, and San Francisco: Kodansha International, 1982. Excellent biographical examination of Bashō's works.

Ueda, Makoto. *Modern Japanese Poets and the Nature of Literature*. Stanford: Stanford University Press, 1983. Essential.

Varley, H. Paul. *Japanese Culture*. Honolulu: University of Hawaii Press, 1984. An excellent introductory textbook.

Waddell, Norman, trans. *The Unborn: Life and Teaching of Bankei*. San Francisco: North Point Press, 1984. Excellent.

Waley, Arthur, and Percy Lund. *Japanese Poetry: The "Uta."* London: Humphries & Co., Ltd.; Rutland, Vermont, and Tokyo: Charles E. Tuttle Company, 1965. Excellent.

Watson, Burton, trans. *Grass Hill: Poems and Prose of the Japanese Monk Gensei*. New York: Columbia University Press, 1983. Burton Watson deserves a Nobel Prize. His translations are a monumental accomplishment.

Watson, Burton. *Japan: First Impressions, Second Thoughts*. Tokyo: Shubun International Co., Ltd., 1984. Revised edition released as *The Rainbow World: Japan in Essays and Translations*. Seattle: Broken Moon Press, 1989. The author has spent most of the past forty years in Japan; a lovely little book.

Watson, Burton, trans. *Ryōkan: Zen Monk-Poet of Japan*. New York: Columbia University Press, 1977. Essential.

Watson, Burton, and Hiroaki Sato, ed. and trans. *From the Country of Eight Islands: An Anthology of Japanese Poetry*. Introduction by

Thomas Rimer. Seattle: University of Washington Press, 1981. *The* great master-anthology.

Watts, Alan W. *The Way of Zen.* New York: Vintage Books, 1957. A classic introduction to Zen.

Wilson, William Scott, trans. *The Unfettered Mind: Writings of Takuan Soho.* Tokyo, New York, and San Francisco: Kodansha International, 1986. Important sixteenth-century Zen master, poet, and calligrapher, famous for the pickle named for him.

The World of Shinto. Tokyo: Bukkyo Dendo Kyokai, 1985. Very good.

Wright, Harold, trans. *The Selected Poems of Shuntaro Tanikawa.* San Francisco: North Point Press, 1983. Very good.

Yampolsky, Philip B., trans. *The Platform Sutra of the Sixth Patriarch.* New York: Columbia University Press, 1967. Excellent commentary and translation.

Yampolsky, Philip B., trans. *Zen Master Hakuin.* New York: Columbia University Press, 1971. An essential book on this very important figure.

Yasunari, Kawabata. *Japan the Beautiful and Myself.* Translated by E. G. Seidensticker. Tokyo, New York, and San Francisco: Kodansha International, 1969. The great novelist's Nobel Prize acceptance speech; magnificent.

Yuasa, Nobuyuki, trans. *The Year of My Life: A Translation of Issa's Oraga Haru (a haibun autobiography).* Berkeley, Los Angeles, and London: University of California Press, 1972. Essential.

About the Author

Sam Hamill was born in 1942, probably somewhere in northern California. Abandoned in northern Utah during World War Two, he spent the war years in an orphanage before being adopted by a Utah farm family. Most of his adolescent years were spent in and out of jails and living on the streets. In his late teens, he enlisted in the U.S. Marine Corps in order to expunge his juvenile record and to see Japan. While serving on the island of Okinawa, he began studying Zen Buddhist literature and became a Conscientious Objector. During the 1960s, he was a civil rights activist and opposed the war in Viet Nam, campaigning for the California State Assembly in 1968 on a democratic-socialist platform. He attended Los Angeles Valley College and the University of California, Santa Barbara. He has served as editor at Copper Canyon Press since 1972, and lives with his partner, Tree Swenson, in a hand-built house near Port Townsend, Washington. He has taught in prisons, public schools, and universities, worked as an advocate for domestic violence programs, and has translated poetry from classical Chinese, Japanese, Latin, and Estonian. He has been awarded a National Endowment for the Arts Fellowship, a Guggenheim Fellowship, a Pacific Northwest Booksellers Award, the Japan–U.S. Fellowship, and a Pushcart Prize. Broken Moon Press will publish his literary essays, *A Poet's Work: The Other Side of Poetry,* in 1990.

Design by John D. Berry. Text set in Bembo on a digital Linotron 202 by Wilsted & Taylor, Oakland, California. Drop initials hand set in Castellar by Mackenzie-Harris Corp., San Francisco, California. Printed on acid-free paper and Smyth sewn in signatures by Malloy Lithographing, Inc., Ann Arbor, Michigan.